The
Touch
OF
Jesus

Discovery House Publishers

Books, music, and videos that feed the soul with the Word of God

Box 3566 Grand Rapids, MI 49501

The Touch OF Jesus

STORIES OF FAITH
FROM THE LIFE OF CHRIST

H.S. VIGEVENO

Discovery House Publishers is affiliated with RBC Ministries, Grand Rapids, Michigan 49512

Discovery House books are distributed to the trade by Thomas Nelson Publishers, Nashville, Tennessee 37214

Scripture taken from the Holy Bible, *New International Version.* Copyright © 1973, 1978, 1984 by International Bible Society. Used by permission of Zondervan Publishing House.

Library of Congress Cataloging-in-Publication Data

Vigeveno, H. S.
    The touch of Jesus : stories of faith from the life of Christ / H. S. Vigeveno.
      p. cm.
    ISBN 1-57293-024-1
    1. Jesus Christ—Miracles. 2. Faith—Biblical teaching. 3. Bible stories, English—N.T. Gospels. I. Title.
BT366.V54   1997
232.9'5—dc21

          97-14645
          CIP

97 99 01 02 00 98
/ CHG /
1 3 5 7 9 10 8 6 4 2

Contents

Introduction

Years ago I heard a preacher say, "Everything Jesus touched He changed." Because of that simple statement, I found myself reading the Gospels in a new light. With excitement I discovered that the lame walk, the blind see, the lost are found, the dead are raised to life, and, most important of all, their lives are changed.

Everything—and everyone—Jesus touched He changed.

Jesus changed the meaning of crucifixion. In His dying He was despised, wounded, and humiliated, but through His agony He turned that cross into a symbol of salvation! Then by rising from the dead He defeated death and removed our fears. Jesus made real the hope of eternal life.

The touching and changing did not stop with the events and people recorded in the Bible. Consider the saints and the martyrs, the leaders and the followers, the people from every walk of life who have called themselves Christians throughout history! Jesus has influenced every facet of culture and society—the humanities, the sciences, music, art, literature, philosophy, government. Through people He has touched He has left His mark on every field of human endeavor. Human beings touched by our Savior care enough to practice healing arts around the globe, for example.

If everything Jesus touched He changed, then it follows that *He can touch and change you too!* That is the good news for everyone. It is possible to become a new person "in Christ," because Jesus is "the same yesterday, today and forever" (Hebrews 13:8).

This book looks at some of those first faith stories that are on display in the Gospels. These are stories of simple, ordinary, and often forgotten people who experienced dramatic changes through Jesus' touch. These stories fascinate us when we realize that they have an impact for us today! I know I can see myself in many of these faith stories. The Gospels tell what happened, but they don't always give much detail about the effect these events had on the people who experienced these miracles. In retelling these stories, I've tried to imagine how these people felt.

In order to bridge the gap from Bible times to our present culture, I have tried to make these stories live by treating them at least somewhat as if they'd happened today. As the stories unfold you will find Scripture quoted and commented upon. Then, at the end of each chapter, the biblical narrative is printed in full. You may find this Scripture passage valuable for meditation. It is my hope that these faith stories will provide you with new insight.

And so I invite you to share this adventure. If you can identify with some of these folk, you will never be the same! Jesus can touch and change every one of us just as He's transformed others! Right now, at this time in your life, whoever you are, wherever you may be, and whatever your problems, there is hope for you.

1

An Officer and a Gentleman

He would never have chosen to come to this place. Never in his life. Who would choose to live in this hot and dusty country? Who would want to live in this desert land so far away from home? It was so different from the little town where he'd grown up, a friendly village on the Mediterranean. Home was that wonderful, happy place on the Italian Riviera!

His father owned a small fishing boat, and even as a child he was allowed to go out to sea with his dad. How he enjoyed the water, the wind, the gentle rocking, the sunshine! His mother often took him and his younger brother and sister to the beach. They would play for hours in the sand, digging trenches, building castles, and splashing in the shallow waters. He enjoyed the late afternoons as the sun began to set and the little boats returned to the harbor.

During his teens he spent hours at the ocean riding the waves in to shore. In those days there were no surfboards, but he bodysurfed, riding wave after wave—and all of it under the most idyllic weather conditions: the air clean, the sky blue, the sunshine almost perfect—and that the year around.

After graduating, he married his high-school sweetheart, and then he enlisted in the army. He had always wanted to join the army. People respected the Roman army because it had made the empire vast and great. The army had extended the empire north and south and east and west and had never lost a battle! Because of its glorious army, Rome had conquered Europe and the Balkans, overrun the Near East, and landed on the shores of Africa.

He enjoyed military life. He moved up quickly in the ranks and soon advanced to the rank of centurion: commander over a hundred soldiers. For awhile he was stationed in his own country, not far from his hometown, but then he was transferred to this forsaken place in a two-bit eastern country. He'd had to look it up on the map. Some small place. *Capernaum?* Where was that? But you can't choose where the army is going to send you.

Fortunately, he was allowed to take his wife and children with him, and, typical of most Roman citizens, he could afford to have slaves; so he brought along two men who served in his house.

This country was so hot! The sun beat down relentlessly and when the wind blew in from the east, it whipped up the sand into his face. He had never perspired so much. That first summer it seemed as if his clothing clung to him all day long as the sun glared down unmercifully.

And these people were strange, these Jews. He had read about them in school, but his knowledge was very limited. They kept to themselves. They had different customs, strange beliefs, and their clothing was so cumbersome. He felt highly superior to these people, as did most of the civilized world, because they had neither the culture of the Greeks nor the nobility of the Romans. Besides, he belonged to the conquerors, while those Jews were the vanquished.

The longer he lived in their land, the more he realized that they were a very religious people. They believed deeply in their God, a God who created the heavens and the earth—the Maker of everything. All of their actions, so it seemed, were based on a law that this God had given them. Not a bad law, he learned. They could not worship any other gods except the Creator. They could not kill, commit adultery, or steal. They had to observe a special day of the week and certain holy days during the year. This religion was an important part of everything they did from morning till night.

And then there was this man Jesus. The centurion had heard many stories about Him. Jesus lived in the neighboring village of Nazareth and often entered Capernaum, where the Roman officer was stationed on the outskirts. Jesus was more than just a religious Jew; He was reported to have healed people. They came to Him in droves and He was able to do wonderful miracles for them. Surely He possessed spiritual powers. The officer had never actually heard or seen Jesus, but the next time he returned to Capernaum from his travels around Galilee, perhaps he would listen and observe.

The next time—but then something unforeseen happened that made the centurion act immediately.

One of his slaves, who had served the centurion's parents, had been given to him when he married. This slave was there when the centurion's children were born, and when the officer was transferred to Israel, this slave came along. He was a trusted member of the family. And now he was very sick. He had hurt his back and couldn't even get out of bed. The slightest movement sent a stab of pain throughout his body. There seemed to be little hope for his recovery, even though he was not yet an old man.

What of this Jesus? Maybe He could do something—but *would* he do something? The centurion had heard about people whom Jesus had miraculously delivered from their afflictions, but what about this case? Neither the centurion nor his slave were Jews. Would that man from Nazareth cure a non-Jew? The centurion hoped so.

When Jesus had entered Capernaum, the centurion came to him, asking him for help. "Lord," he said, "my servant lies at home paralyzed and in terrible suffering." Jesus said to him, "I will go and heal him."

Really? Come and heal his Roman slave? Just like that? The fact that he was both a Roman and a slave made no difference?

During the centurion's brief stay among the Jews, he had learned that their religion did not allow them to enter non-Jewish homes! They could not eat meals with people who were not Jews. That is why none of these people had ever come into the centurion's house. Because of the Jews' religious laws, they looked down on the Romans and on all foreigners. They believed that they were chosen by their God, that they were more holy than other people, and they didn't associate with non-Jews.

How ironic! If only they knew how the Romans regarded them and looked down on them! And so did the Greeks. If only the Jews could hear those conversations in Rome and Athens and throughout the empire!

Why then would Jesus be willing to cross lines and enter the centurion's house? Surely Jesus was aware of the stigma, as well as the religious customs of His people. This would never be acceptable! That is why the centurion decided to spare Jesus the embarrassment. He would simply not invite Him.

The centurion replied, "Lord, I do not deserve to have you come under my roof."

He was a Roman citizen, an officer in the prestigious, conquering army. As a Roman he considered himself a master of the world, superior to other races and nations. And these Jews were not even Roman citizens! They were beneath him. But this Jesus was not just a member of a minority race. He was surely superior to ordinary people. He demonstrated a power that set Him apart, a power that could cure sickness and disease. The power of God was in Him. Because of Jesus' divine power the centurion felt unworthy.

Another thought kept the centurion from inviting Jesus into his house: Jesus might be embarrassed. He knew that these Jews lived in small, very simple hovels. One room served as living room, kitchen, and bedroom. They were a poor people. And for Jesus to walk into his spacious three-bedroom house with servant quarters would be humiliating. Furthermore, on display in his living room stood some expensive Italian marble, wedding gifts from his grandparents. Two exquisite Persian rugs brightened up the room. No, it would be inappropriate to invite Jesus into his home.

But there was something else. "Lord, I do not deserve to have you come under my roof. But just say the word, and my servant will be healed. For I myself am a man under authority, with soldiers under me. I tell this one, 'Go,' and he goes, and that one, 'Come,' and he comes. I say to my servant, 'Do this,' and he does it."

He had learned this much in the military: commands are to be obeyed. No ifs, ands, or buts. When a superior officer gives an order to a slave or soldier, he must act on it without any hesitation. That was the way the military operated. As simple as that.

In a similar way Jesus seems to have certain powers. When he issues a command it will be obeyed. Those reported "cures" are the result of Jesus' authority. He simply commands a disease to leave the body, and the illness vanishes! When he gives orders to demons, the demons depart. This the centurion had heard. And if that authority is genuine, then Jesus does not have to accompany him to his house at all. That would be unnecessary. He has merely to issue the order and the slave will be miraculously healed.

When Jesus heard this, he was astonished and said to those following him, "I tell you the truth, I have not found anyone in Israel with such great faith."

Really? What is this thing about "faith"? The centurion didn't know he had "faith." That's just the way it is in the military. You give orders. And you take orders. Isn't that the way the world operates? So, if Jesus is someone who is above the lame and the paralyzed, then He can command any disorder to leave. That's how it works. Now if that is considered faith, he had never thought of it that way. It's just common sense. Is that what faith is? Common sense? Is that what it means to believe in the Jewish God, or in any god? He was not really a religious man, but now he was informed that he had faith? was honored for his faith?

And Jesus went on: "Many will come from the east and the west and will take their places at the feast with Abraham, Isaac, and Jacob in the kingdom of heaven.

But the subjects of the kingdom will be thrown outside into the darkness, where there will be weeping and gnashing of teeth."

Who are those guys? He had never heard of them. Abraham, Isaac, and Jacob? He would have to find out about them, because if they are in the kingdom of heaven, he would need to know more about them! And who are those "subjects of the kingdom" who will be thrown out? They belong to the kingdom, don't they? Why will they be thrown out? Because they lack faith? Faith in what? Faith in God? Faith in a divine order? Faith in power? Faith in Jesus of Nazareth? Is faith the issue here?

But if all this is true, how do you get faith in God? Does ordering slaves about have anything to do with faith? Is that the same thing? Is that what Jesus thinks? Jesus says that he, the centurion, has more faith than many of those pious Jews. But how could that be? He was just a military man. He didn't really know what to make of this faith thing.

Nor did he like to hear about these penalties. Weeping? Grinding of teeth? Darkness? Remaining outside in fear instead of inside in joy? That had an ominous sound to it. Does this God of the Jews punish? For what? For not believing? Is faith the issue here? Is there a punishment for missing something, a judgment to come?

The other day he'd overheard some people talking about the words of Jesus in the street. Jesus had evidently mentioned these penalties, this darkness, and these teeth before. They were discussing the coming judgment, and someone asked specifically about the grinding of teeth. "What if a person dies and comes to the judgment without any teeth?" And another replied, "Teeth will be provided!"

But this was no laughing matter. So he would make it into the kingdom, just because he had shown a little faith? Was that all there was to it? Was that enough? And others would not make it into the kingdom because they lacked this faith?

Jesus said to the centurion, "Go! It will be done for you just as you believed it would."

As he believes? Just like that? Is that it? Is that all there is? Should he just leave now? Jesus ordered him to go home. That was a command. And a command must be obeyed. Would his slave be sick or well? Don't ask any questions. Just go. Go home.

His servant was healed at that very hour! That was all there was to it. As simple as that. When he returned to his house, the slave greeted him at the front door, smiling. He was well! It was a miracle. All the pain gone, the affliction healed, the man was back on his feet. The centurion could not help but give his trusted servant a hug. It was highly unusual for a master to hug a slave, but he couldn't help himself. It felt right somehow. Because of his faith!

That evening at the dinner table as the slave came through the kitchen door to serve the dinner, his children asked their father how their servant had been healed so quickly, so miraculously. How had it happened? The officer smiled and told the story. It was then that he insisted they would go as a family to listen to the teaching of this Jesus. Either tomorrow or the next day, but soon. He wanted to learn more from this Man of God. His first encounter was only the beginning. From now on he would gladly join the audience whenever Jesus was in town.

What is faith? What is believing? In a world that operates completely without faith in God, what does it mean to believe in God? The world is dominated by politics and economics, by fluctuating interest rates and stocks and mutual funds. God's Word is not considered pivotal in the realms of technology, science, communications, and computers, nor within the environment of industrial giants, large corporations, or military build-up and aggression. Is God ever mentioned where you work, play, sleep, and eat, and live each day? You can live very well without ever having to consider faith. Some people think about faith only for an hour in church. The rest of time it's business as usual in our secular society.

This secular, materialistic, realistic way of life hangs like heavy clouds over the landscape. It obscures the spiritual. It conceals reality. The only way to break through that oppressive layer is by faith. As a plane taking off emerges into the sunshine above an oppressive cloud cover, faith gets us through the material and the secular into the presence of God. To believe is to make contact with the God who rules the universe! Faith is more than a need I have here below; it is an arrow that reaches beyond and touches the eternal, sovereign, almighty God.

God's Word says that the Creator of the universe draws near to us. He has penetrated the cloud cover to enter our materialistic, secular, pleasure-seeking world. He has come into our midst in the person of Jesus—"Immanuel"—God with us. He is not only in heaven, He is also on earth. The kingdom of God is among you.

When we first begin to live by faith, it may seem as if faith doesn't accomplish much. What does faith achieve? Are prayers answered? Are we heard? Does it make any difference that we believe? We hear almost nothing. We see very few changes. We may not feel much of anything. And yet we go on believing and praying and trusting. We persevere in spite of all opposition, doubts, and fears. Sometimes our prayers don't get answered for a long time. That tests our faith, but in the meantime we're still talking to God. We hold on somehow. We keep on believing. We refuse to give up easily.

Maybe one day we will be able to testify with Gordon MacDonald, who writes in his latest book something very remarkable: "I know now that God has never been oblivious of one word I've spoken from the soul in his direction" (Gordon MacDonald, *The Life God Blessed* [Nashville, Nelson Publishers, 1994], 203).

That is an amazing expression of faith! Such faith is built on the firm conviction that God is God—that God can be trusted, believed in, relied upon. It is a simple faith; it is also a strong faith.

Faith also requires that you act on it. Faith is not passive, a kind of sit-back-and-relax attitude. Don't expect all kind of evidence before you are willing to trust God. Come as you are. Come with your fears, your doubts, your questions, your shortcomings—even your shame. Come and know that you are welcome!

And don't complicate faith. Jesus says that faith is very simple. He points out that people themselves have sufficient faith within to make them whole. Most people are not even aware that they possess this power. "The word is near you, . . . in your heart" (Romans 10:8). That is the word of faith.

The Roman officer did not realize that. Jesus pointed it out to him. It is "as you believed" that things happen. The centurion had already shifted common experience into a spiritual realm, and Jesus congratulated him on his practical faith.

As a military man he reasoned that you must obey a command. Carrying out an order turns faith into action. Faith is a matter of acting on a promise! You may not think of that as faith, but that is exactly something faith does!

If you have been in the armed services, you can relate. You know what authority is all about. But maybe you have never lived under such a structure. So, let's consider something else.

Do you go to the bank? I see you there, every week or two, depositing your paycheck. You do that without the slightest hesitation. You have complete trust in the bank. In fact some of our banks even carry the words *savings* and *trust* in their titles—religious terms! You believe they will take your hard-earned money and post it to your account—not to someone else's. You trust the teller to do it right, that he or she will not pocket your paycheck. You believe the computer will record it correctly. You believe the people working in the bank will be faithful to their tasks, the bank will guard your money, and in the process will not go bankrupt. And they will even give your money back to you when you ask for it.

You rely on the bank enough to put *all* your hard-earned money there for deposit. You don't stack anything away somewhere else, just in case. You have complete trust in the system, even though you have read about embezzlement, inside jobs, bank failures, and bankruptcies.

My old bank is no more. The superstructure toppled and all the branches failed. That bank was taken over by another conglomerate. But I still deposit my money in that same bank building. I don't sock anything away under my mattress. Banking requires faith. It is a matter of trust. When I punch my secret code into the ATM, I always get back the right amount of cash.

If I deposit my money into the bank, can I also deposit my faith in God? Can I trust God to hear my requests? When I sign a check with my name and it is honored, do I believe that petitions in the name of Jesus will be honored too, especially if I ask sincerely, in the spirit of the teaching and person of Jesus? Can I transfer my ordinary banking actions to the spiritual realm? Am I able to learn to trust God without reserve? Can I believe His promises and act on them? Is it true that I can ask *anything* as long as it is in harmony with His Spirit? Do I have that kind of faith?

That's exactly what the centurion exemplified. He reasoned from his military context and translated that to an area he didn't understand, the spiritual. And Jesus praised him for it! Jesus even announced this to the world and pointed to the examples of those respected Jewish fathers—Abraham, Isaac, and Jacob.

Is it possible that the officer felt good, after all, that he had been transferred to this forsaken desert country among a people he had never considered very important or influential? Is it possible that he learned from his one encounter with Jesus something that deeply affected his life and future? Perhaps that single experience of healing power for his poor, ordinary slave touched and changed him completely.

Let me add a footnote to this story. God rewards faith. The heroes of the Bible who are paraded before us in the eleventh chapter of Hebrews, have one thing in common. They all lived by faith. The writer introduces each one with the same words: "By faith . . . ." The reason they are grouped in this way is that they believed, just as did other faith-heroes, beginning with Abel at the dawn of history.

These heroes include such greats as Abraham, Moses, Gideon, David, Daniel, and the prophets. They have overcome the world. And if we extend the list, must we not now also include the centurion from Rome? Yes. This officer and gentleman expressed a greater faith than did the Jewish people among whom he lived! According to Jesus he is right up there with Abraham, Isaac, and Jacob!

And that means that if we were to extend that listing throughout history, you, too can belong to that great company of believers! When you put your faith in Jesus Christ as Lord and Savior, you enter that family called the "great cloud of witnesses." And to what do they give witness? *That they live by faith in a world without it.* They endure life's trials and troubles by looking to Jesus, the Pioneer and Perfecter of our faith. They seek a city that has foundations, whose Maker and Builder is God.

So may Jesus be able to say of you, "I have not found such faith, no not among my own people." May it be true of you as it was for the officer and gentleman from Italy who found his servant well at home, *"as you have believed."*

> When Jesus had entered Capernaum, a centurion came to him, asking for help. "Lord," he said, "my servant lies at home paralyzed and in terrible suffering."
>
> Jesus said to him, "I will go and heal him."
>
> The centurion replied, "Lord, I do not deserve to have you come under my roof. But just say the word, and my servant will be healed. For I myself am a man under authority, with soldiers under me. I tell this one, 'Go,' and he goes; and that one, 'Come,' and he comes. I say to my servant, 'Do this,' and he does it."
>
> When Jesus heard this, he was astonished, and said to those following him, "I tell you the truth, I have not found anyone in Israel

with such faith. I say to you that many will come from the east and the west, and will take their places at the feast with Abraham, Isaac and Jacob in the kingdom of heaven. But the subjects of the kingdom will be thrown outside, into the darkness, where there will be weeping and gnashing of teeth."

Then Jesus said to the centurion, "Go! It will be done just as you believed it would." And his servant was healed at that very hour.

Matthew 8:5

2

A Man Possessed

He lived alone. He had no friends. Well, he knew a few people, but he could not consider them friends—acquaintances perhaps. He had never married, had dated only occasionally. He knew he was different from other people, and it made him feel isolated. He realized this isolation from others also made him a stranger to himself. He didn't know who he was, really. And worst of all he felt far away from God.

When he went into the village, people locked their gates and doors. Some people screamed at him when he walked through town. Children hurled insults. Their parents cursed him. How then could he survive? He scrounged for food in the wilderness—killed small animals, ate whatever he could find. He took fewer and fewer trips to the town market. What was the point? At least they left him alone out here among the tombs. No one talked down to him here. No one condemned him here. But his life was forlorn, because he was so terribly alone in the world.

This man lived in the tombs, and no one could bind him any more, not even with a chain. For he had often been chained hand and foot, but he tore the chains apart and broke the irons on his feet. No one was strong enough to subdue him.

He was possessed—demon-possessed. Everything about him was wrong, foul, and bad. He didn't know what made him wander into town without any clothes on. That's when several men would surround him, throw some clothes on him, and tie him up with chains. The only thing positive about him was his brute physical power. He had the strength of a bear. He was almost Samson all over again, but an uncontrollable Samson. No one would fight him, because he could tear any man apart like he tore apart the chains they tried to clamp on him. These strong chains, sufficient to shackle anyone else, he snapped like thread.

Yet, he needed people in his life—people who cared, people who would befriend him. He had feelings too, just like everyone else. If only one person would accept him, would try to understand him. But no one ever asked, "How are you doing? Are you okay? What are you going to do today?" He had no one to laugh with or cry with or walk with or eat with. No wonder he felt so alienated from God, too.

Life was unbearable. During the day he wandered about, observing everything in nature, rocks and mountains, trees and bushes, the sky, the sand. He learned from wild animals and insect life—could sit for hours watching the ants. He pondered the wind, the rain, the blistering sun, and the ever-changing clouds. He wondered about normal people. Sometimes he roamed about naked, forgetting even to cover himself. He could not find peace in his soul.

Uncontrollable thoughts, evil thoughts, plagued him day and night. He couldn't sleep. He scurried about at night, his mind racing with angry, wild thoughts that never allowed him to stop. Terrible, fearful dreams haunted him. He often woke up after a crazy dream only to discover that he was bleeding somewhere. He didn't know how he had cut himself, except for the sharp stone lying by his side.

For the French atheist Jean Paul Sartre, "Hell is other people." For the Swedish filmmaker Ingmar Bergman, "Hell is being alone."

If only this possessed man could have dialed 911 like other people. At least the paramedics would get to know him. They recognize those regulars who call 911, who seem to have one "emergency" after another. They have an accident or cut themselves. They say they can't help it, but some seem to do it deliberately, as if they are eager for attention, these 911 junkies. Many of them live on welfare with nothing to do. Perhaps they are possessed in some way too?

> When he saw Jesus from a distance, he ran and fell on his knees in front of him. He shouted at the top of his voice, "What do you want with me, Jesus, Son of the Most High God? Swear to God that you won't torture me!"

How did this reject from society know about Jesus? How did this antisocial, forgotten, and forsaken nobody figure out that the one who had just walked ashore in his country was the Son of the Most High God? Did his demons inform Him? For it is clear in Scripture that the demons know who Jesus is! How else could this poor fellow approach Jesus with fear and trembling: "Swear . . . that you won't torture me!" Why should this lonely tomb dweller, who could subdue the strongest Sumo wrestler or knock out the boxing heavyweight champion of the world, cower and cringe before Jesus of Nazareth?

He lived in a world he could not understand; so do we. He was tormented by spiritual wickedness that overpowered him, and so often that's our experience. Do we recognize the evil forces in our society? Are we aware of demonic influences that infiltrate government, economics, commerce, and law? Have we ever tried to do something that seemed honest and right, only to be informed that we cannot do that because some law forbids it? Evil forces pervade our culture.

Something had driven the possessed man to the feet of Jesus, and Jesus asked him, "What is your name?"

What is my name? Lonely, that's me! I have no friends, I'm all alone. That's who I am. I'm confused and a little bit crazy. I lose control and I make myself bleed. I get down on myself. I don't have a good self-image. I'm so angry, I can't stand it any more. I'm fed up. I'm hopeless. My life is intolerable.

What is my name? I'm annoyed. I'm troubled. I'm afraid. I'm discouraged. I can't get rid of my demon. I'm a hapless victim. I come from a dysfunctional family. I can't cope. That's who I am. Now you know my name. I'm a sinner and I'm filled with disgust and shame because of my sins.

"My name is Legion," he replied, "for we are many."

I'm Legion. I'm a whole Roman squadron! There are so many of us. It's not just one or two worrisome sins. I'm full of sins, I can't count them any more. I fight so many battles, you have no idea. You can't possibly know what goes on inside of me.

I'm sick of the struggle. I can't win. I'm a loser. I'm a victim. I'm possessed. My name is Legion.

Jesus said to him, "Come out of this man, you evil spirit!"

Do we realize that only the power of God can overcome evil powers? If disease and sickness are brought
on by the very existence of evil in the world, do we see
that Jesus has come to battle that evil? Jesus has authority over disease and death. He alone can cast out
demons! He has divine power over all evil forces. Jesus
demonstrates God's reign among us, the triumph of
righteousness. "If I drive out demons by the Spirit of
God, then the kingdom of God has come upon you"
(Matthew 12:28).

Can we also rest assured that Jesus has never left us
or forsaken us? that He still owns this power today?
that He is the same today as He was yesterday and as He
will be forever? that He has sent us the Holy Spirit to be
with us till the very end?

> He begged Jesus again and again not
> to send them out of the area.
> A great herd of pigs was feeding on the
> nearby hillside. The demons begged Jesus,
> "Send us among the pigs; allow us to go
> into them." He gave them permission, and
> the evil spirits came out of the man and
> went into the pigs. The herd, about two
> thousand in number, rushed down the
> steep bank into the lake and were
> drowned.

How many demons did he have? Two thousand pigs
rush into the sea because of one possessed man? Unbelievable!

What were all those pigs doing on the other side of
the sea of Galilee? Were these pigs raised to be

slaughtered and sold for bacon, pork, and ham only
in that country, or did some of that meat slip across
the border to the Israelites? Surely two thousand pigs
so near the border arouse suspicion. The Jews had
been forbidden to eat pork, so why were those hogs
being raised there? And now that whole herd runs
into the sea? Those demons overpower all those hogs?
Can you even begin to imagine the economic disaster
for the pig farmers? The loss in thousands of shekels
(or dollars)?

Those tending the pigs ran off and reported this in the town and countryside,
and the people went out to see what had
happened.

When they came to Jesus, they saw the
man who had been possessed by the legion
of demons sitting there dressed and in his
right mind, and they were afraid.

Those who had seen it told the people
what had happened to the demon-possessed man—and told about the pigs as
well.

"How can this possessed maniac be
cured? Why does he suddenly seem normal?"

"That doesn't make sense. How can
anyone explain this change?"

"Some evil power possessed this poor
soul, and who could deliver him from his
predicament? Only the power of God!"

"But is this really the power of God?
Can such people ever change?"

"You don't mean to tell me that this man from Galilee can do something like that? He is not God."

"So, who is he anyway? some magic man? someone in touch with mysterious powers?"

They were afraid. For years they had feared the brute force of this demonic strongman, and now they feared the spiritual forces that had made him whole. Unquestionably, he was healed. Jesus had transformed him into a person who was meek, mild, and manageable for the first time in his life, and they were afraid of the power that had made those demons depart begging and screaming.

It was better before—in the good old days. It would really be much better to leave him alone, this madman living among the tombs. The Gerasenes seemed to be more interested in the pig phenomenon than in the salvation of this possessed loner. All they could think about was the loss of the swine, not the gain of one human soul.

And we're very much the same. We want to see and hear and read sensational news in the papers and magazines. Give us the latest about famous people. We tune in the lurid tales on *Hard Copy* and *Inside Edition*. We buy those scandal sheets at supermarket check-outs, while the good news of people redeemed from their awful demons doesn't get any publicity. We're not really interested in a good-news story about some crazy man from the tombs.

"Forget all the evildoers in the world. Don't try to deliver them from their sinful ways. There will always be panhandlers, pimps and prostitutes, gangsters and gun-crazed mobsters, addicts and alcoholics. Just leave them all alone. Let them wallow in their guilt and sin—and go back across the lake where you belong. We don't really want you here, messing around with our country." The people began to plead with Jesus to leave their region.

"Stick to your preaching over there on the other side of the lake. It's safe to preach in your synagogues in Galilee and forget about us. The truth is that we would rather tolerate the evil that destroys sinners than allow our economy to be turned upside down!"

"The economy is doing very well the way it is, as long as the pig business is thriving. So leave well enough alone."

"Furthermore, you have no right to destroy our property. Who are you to tamper with someone else's possessions? Those pigs belong to us, not to you. You're a stranger here. Who do you think you are, to ruin our profit and run those hogs into the sea? Get out of here, you pseudosavior. Stop interfering with our livelihood."

We'd rather have drugs and alcoholism and red-light districts and rape than permit the stock market to crash. We'd rather endure crime in the city and build a tougher police force or more prisons than see our business world come apart.

Those who grow tobacco or deal in illicit drugs or sell illegal weapons or offer prostitution and pornography—or raise pigs—don't want any interference in the way they make a living. They don't want anything to upset their livelihood. They don't want anyone to preach about the economy, right or wrong. They don't want spiritual interference. The church doesn't have any right to stick its nose into their business. What you do inside the church doesn't bother the world. You can say anything you want in your church, but when you take away our right to raise pigs, you'd better look out. There's trouble ahead, because that kind of preaching is meddling.

Little did they, or we, realize that one soul is worth more than two thousand pigs. One soul is worth more than the most thriving economy or the most financially successful enterprise in the world. One human soul is more valuable than the stock market. That's the choice we are asked to make between God and materialism. We cannot serve both masters.

> As Jesus was getting into the boat, the man who had been demon-possessed begged to go with him. Jesus did not let him but said, "Go home to your family and tell them how much the Lord has done for you and how he has had mercy on you." So the man went away and began to tell in the

Decapolis how much Jesus had done for
him.

Sometimes I have trouble accepting the teaching of
Jesus, too. I don't like the way Jesus does things. Why
should this possessed, tormented outcast be allowed to
receive the mercy of God, the same as me? He was a
menace to society before his salvation, and is he now
awarded a place in paradise, along with me? As long as
grace is extended to me and forgiveness covers my sins,
I won't object. But what if the evil people in the world,
the addicts and adulterers and criminals and out-and-
out sinners—yes, the trash of society—are allowed to
participate in the good news also? What about rapists or
murderers who have never lived a Christian life who
beg to be forgiven at the last minute? Will they be rewarded with heaven, the same as I?

Jesus tells a story about a man who needs people to
work in his vineyard. He finds eager laborers in the early morning. A couple of hours later he chooses more
good workers. He returns several times, until finally he
invites even the shiftless who hang around city parks,
those who are no longer on welfare and those who stand
around with signs, "Will Work for Food"—but won't
when you ask them. And then at the end of the day, he
first pays those no-goods who were out there for only an
hour or so and gives them a full day's pay! He has the
audacity to pay the bums and shiftless exactly the same
wages he has promised me? But I've been working all
day long in the hot sun! Doesn't that count for anything? My problem begins not with those others but with
me. My problem starts when I discover they are awarded the same privileges that I am.

It's like another story Jesus tells about a father with two sons. The younger runs off with his share of the inheritance while the older son keeps the business going. He works every day conscientiously, dedicated and committed. When the younger brother returns after years of reckless living, their father throws a big party. But the reliable, dutiful older son refuses to come. Why should he? Why should he attend a party for a brother who has partied all those years he has conscientiously slaved for his father? Why should he come to another party for party boy who has been partying his life away?

A woman went back to her church one Sunday after her divorce had been final for some time. She sat in her usual place near the back. And there, close to the front, worshiped her former husband, a doctor, who had an affair with a young nurse, to whom he was now married. At the close of the service when the pastor gave an invitation to join the church, the doctor and his new wife went forward. And the first wife said to herself, there in the back pew, "If God receives them, I'm never coming back to church again. Not ever!" And she didn't. We can sympathize with her pain, but is this a worthy reaction?

Amazing grace is not for everybody, is it? Amazing grace is not to be handed out to those who live in the tombs? Amazing grace is not for those who gamble and lose all their money? Amazing grace is not for those who persecute the church and bring Christians into court or throw them in jail? Amazing grace is not for those who sleep around with just about everybody? Amazing grace is not for any of those outcasts of society just because they call on the Lord to be saved? It isn't possible to cry out to Jesus with your dying breath after you have spent your life in sin, is it? Somehow it doesn't seem right, especially when I have worked so hard at my Christianity all my life.

Why does Jesus choose people like the lonely, the poor, the unimportant, the marginal of society? Why doesn't Jesus pick more of the influential, the financially successful, the sports heroes, the movie stars, the celebrities? I want to read their stories. I like to hear about their experiences. I don't really want to know about this unimportant demented madman from the tombs. I'm not really interested in *his* salvation story.

But if Jesus touches people like that, doesn't that mean there is hope for you and for me? That is good news! You and me, with all our blemishes, with all our failures, with all our defeats? Yes, we may even be possessed too. Is there something I can't control in my life—a wrongful passion, a degrading habit, some repeated, shameful behavior? Are you defeated again and again by evil thoughts? We wrestle not only against flesh and blood, but against demons that possess our souls. Now we can have hope because of this powerful conversion.

In our culture, with addicts and victims and tortured souls, how can we not recognize that many in our society are possessed, too? Talk with any redeemed alcoholic who has found a new life, any drug addict who has finally been freed from her or his habit, any struggling, desperate soul in a recovery program, and you will discover that all readily admit they have been possessed. But now they are free!

Jesus calls sinners to repentance. No one is excluded. All are welcome, from the highest to the lowest, from the greatest to the smallest—no matter how overwhelming the addiction, no matter how terrible the failure, no matter what sin has been committed. Jesus honors the confession and repentance of anyone, no matter what country or race or way of life. He will go into the highways and byways and compel us to come in! He wants us to receive salvation and holy health.

I may balk when amazing grace is freely handed out to everyone else, people who, in my opinion, don't deserve it. But can I be sure that *I* deserve it? Here is a marvelous statement from one of the most respected, humble saints of the Christian church, a man who lived in the twelfth century.

> We have learned that every soul, even if it is loaded down with sins, ensnared in vices, trapped by the enticement of pleasure, a captive in exile . . . enslaved by cares, distracted with business, shrinking with fear, afflicted with griefs, astray in errors, troubled by anxieties, disturbed by suspicions, . . . counted with those who go down to hell—we have learned that every soul, even thus condemned and thus despairing, can turn back and find that it cannot only breathe the hope of forgiveness and mercy, but even dare to aspire to be the Bride of the Word, when it is not afraid to make alliance with God and to take on the sweet yoke of love with the King of the angels.
> —*Bernard of Clairveaux*

This pathetic, possessed person is now sitting there in his right mind with Jesus. Everything previous was wrong. Every other way of life was wrong. Only what Jesus has done for him is right. He is no longer under the influence of evil. He is controlled by the living God. He has received righteousness, a righteousness not earned by anything he has accomplished. No, he didn't do it for himself. How could he save himself? How could he change his behavior? It was all because of the righteousness bestowed by Jesus.

Salvation is not something you can do for yourself. You know this already. If an evil power has you in its grip, you cannot extricate yourself. You cannot conquer it, because you have been conquered. You have tried again and again, and you have failed. You have battled your temptation and lost. Demon possession is serious business. And only the almighty God who is far above all evil can bring us peace. Only the powerful Lord Jesus can cast out demons. That is what Jesus demonstrates, there in that foreign country on the other side of the Sea of Galilee.

If you don't believe this to be true, then keep on trying to overcome evil by yourself. Keep on in your own strength as long as you can. Go on until you drop at the finish line, spent, exhausted, and completely defeated. After all those efforts you may admit, "I can't do this by myself." Then you will be ready to turn to Jesus.

You can spare yourself all that effort and all that misery. Come to Jesus now. He can deliver you. "All authority in heaven and on earth has been given to me," Jesus said (Matthew 28:18). All power. He demonstrates that power over and over again during His ministry and throughout history. He has promised to be with us to the end of the age (Matthew 28:20).

Are you in your right mind? You can be. The psalmist says, "I am still confident of this: I will see the goodness of the LORD in the land of the living" (Psalm 27:13). Without God he was hopeless, helpless, and in despair, but with God it's a different story.

There is no reason why what happened to this pathetic, possessed loner could not happen to you right now!

> They went across the lake to the region of the Gerasenes. When Jesus got out of the boat, a man with an evil spirit came from the tombs to meet him. This man lived in the tombs, and no one could bind him any more, not even with a chain. For he had often been chained hand and foot, but he tore the chains apart and broke the irons on his feet. No one was strong enough to subdue him. Night and day among the tombs and in the hills he would cry out and cut himself with stones.
>
> When he saw Jesus from a distance, he ran and fell on his knees in front of him. He shouted at the top of his voice, "What do you want with me, Jesus, Son of the Most High God? Swear to God that you won't torture me!" For Jesus had said to him, "Come out of this man, you evil spirit!"
>
> Then Jesus asked him, "What is your name?"
>
> "My name is Legion," he replied, "for we are many." And he begged Jesus again and again not to send them out of the area.

A large herd of pigs was feeding on the nearby hillside. The demons begged Jesus, "Send us among the pigs; allow us to go into them." He gave them permission, and the evil spirits came out and went into the pigs. The herd, about two thousand in number, rushed down the steep bank into the lake and were drowned.

Those tending the pigs ran off and reported this in the town and countryside, and the people went out to see what had happened. When they came to Jesus, they saw the man who had been possessed by the legion of demons, sitting there, dressed and in his right mind; and they were afraid. Those who had seen it told the people what had happened to the demon-possessed man—and told about the pigs as well. Then the people began to plead with Jesus to leave the region.

As Jesus was getting into the boat, the man who had been demon-possessed begged to go with him. Jesus did not let him, but said, "Go home to your family and tell them how much the Lord has done for you and how he has had mercy on you." So the man went away and began to tell in the Decapolis how much Jesus had done for him. And all the people were amazed.

Mark 5:1

ℬ

Daddy's Girl

One of the synagogue rulers, named Jairus, came. He was a prominent man in town. He was known for his honesty in business and as a person who could be trusted. Since he served on the board of ruling elders in the synagogue, he enjoyed prestige in the community. Jairus took his religion seriously. But seeing Jesus, he fell at His feet!

Why would this respected elder humiliate himself and fall prostrate at Jesus' feet? Citizens of means and importance do not disgrace themselves in public. Oh, some poor beggar might crawl for a handout. Lowly, uneducated people down on their luck might degrade themselves, but not an esteemed elder like Jairus. Besides, the Jews consider the worship of human beings idolatry, and idolatry is strictly forbidden. Worship belongs only to God!

Why, then does Jairus humble himself? He did not know much about Jesus. He had not heard Jesus say "I am the Son of God," because Jesus didn't go around telling people that He was the Messiah. He waited until people discovered it for themselves.

Jairus knew only that Jesus was a prophet, a worker of miracles, a person with divine power. He had heard stories about Jesus' ability to heal the sick. He knew that Jesus spoke words of wisdom and truth, but that was hardly enough for this humbling abasement. No, what brought him to Jesus was a personal problem. Jairus was up against something beyond his control. He was really hurting!

> Seeing Jesus, Jairus fell at his feet and pleaded earnestly with him, "My little daughter is dying."
>
> My little girl is terribly ill, and I can't do anything to help her. I've prayed about it, but my prayers don't seem to reach God. They have not been answered. I want to have faith, but that's not easy because nothing happens. I've taken her to the doctor, who's given her some medicine, but it hasn't helped and the doctor doesn't know what else to try. Now she's feverish and clammy. She's lost her color. She's getting weaker and sometimes she moans quietly in pain. And she is only twelve years old, my little girl. What can I do?

Parents feel so helpless when children fall ill. But in those days Jewish people tended to believe that diseases were deserved. They expected to suffer because they felt unworthy. Affliction was considered a punishment from God—not that a twelve-year-old was being punished for her sins—of course not. But what had been amiss in Daddy's life? Where had he failed?

There must be some reason why this trouble has befallen the family.

> Jairus said, "Please come and put your hands on her so that she will be healed and live." You can do something, Jesus. I believe you can do something. Lay your hands on her sick body and she will be healed. Yes, I believe because I love my little girl and I don't want her to die. And I believe you will love her too when you see her. She's so precious. And even though affliction can be a judgment on sin, I believe in a God who does not want people to suffer. He loves her, too, and I know God wants to make her well. Come see for yourself, touch her and she will recover.

How did Jairus get his faith? Why did he believe against all odds? Was it the hopelessness of the situation that made him reach out? the love for his little girl that gave him the courage to believe? From where do you get your faith in a faithless world? From where do you gain faith when you exist in a materialistic society that disregards spiritual reality? This real world is scientific, logical, reasonable.

And faith?

Jairus probably had faith because he was serious about his role in the synagogue. He trusted in the living God and applied his faith to life. He allowed what he believed to spill over into everyday problems, even this awful predicament with his much beloved little girl. That is why he comes to Jesus—because of his faith.

Faith grows when you are with other people who also live by faith. Faith develops when you worship with others who confess their sins and want to draw near to God. Faith ripens when you read the Scriptures and realize what God has done throughout history. Scripture is the record of how God has saved and guided His people in both the Old and the New Testaments. This same God is with you, too!

So Jesus went with him.

Jesus responds to the simple request. He has not objected to Jairus's kneeling before Him, even though that was unorthodox. This incident brings to mind the time when the apostle Peter traveled to see the Roman centurion Cornelius. Cornelius, believing Peter to be an angel from God, prostrated himself before Peter. Peter immediately made him get up, because he, Peter, was an ordinary human being and unworthy of worship. Worship belongs only to God.

Jesus does not object to Jairus's reverence before Him. What is this saying about Jesus?

Quietly, without argument, Jesus is willing to accompany Jairus to his house. He is full of empathy and compassion. He wants to help. This is how Jesus reveals the nature of God. He accepts the worship reserved for God alone and then by His action demonstrates what God is like. God listens. God cares. God is compassionate. God comes to our aid. God is love. Jesus accompanies us to help us cope with adversity.

The procession heading for Jairus's home is suddenly interrupted. A woman emerges from the crowd and touches Jesus' clothing. No one pays any attention to her, but she is instantly healed! Only Jesus realizes what has happened; He stops walking. He questions the disciples, but they throw up their hands. They are not aware of anything unusual. But the woman has heard Jesus' question; she steps forward. They have a conversation about her experience, and during this brief exchange we are likely to forget about Daddy's girl. Suddenly, the bottom drops out of everything.

While Jesus was still speaking, some men came from the house of Jairus. "Your daughter is dead," they said, "Why bother the teacher any more?"

"She's dead. It's all over. Nothing more can be done. Not now."

"She stopped breathing and we closed her eyes. This should never have happened. She was so young."

"She went quietly. Yes, it's a tragedy. She's gone, and there is no reason for Jesus to walk to the house. It's too late."

Jairus is in shock. He can't speak. He can't believe what he has heard. Even though his heart is beating wildly in his chest, he cannot shed any tears. Feelings of sorrow and grief do not surface yet, only shock and denial. *She can't be dead, can she? How can this be? Why did it happen? Why did God not keep her alive until I returned home? I left her side only long enough to get some help from Jesus. Why now? Why did she have to die? She's only twelve years old.*

Ignoring what they said, Jesus told the synagogue ruler, "Don't be afraid; just believe."

Just believe? How can you ignore death? That doesn't make sense at all. That's not real. That's strange. This is a hopeless situation. When she was alive, there was hope. But now that she is gone, hope is dead. Death is the end. How can there be any reversal of death? Death is so grim. Death is so final. Death leaves us no alternative! What do you mean, just believe? Are you serious?

From where did Jesus get His faith? Why did Jesus still entertain hope? What were His resources? Does He trust in God because He is the Son of God? But if He has this faith because He is divine, then He has not fully entered the human race. Scripture teaches that Jesus has become completely human, laying aside all the prerogatives of God, emptying Himself of the glory and the power, to take on the form of a lowly servant. Therefore it is as one human being to another that Jesus tells Jairus to believe. This human Jesus has supreme confidence in His heavenly Father.

Following the tragic death report, Jairus guards whatever glimmer of hope he had before. He believes, even though he is obviously in shock at the bad news.

People in shock are too overcome to reason, argue, or think clearly, so they are likely to go along.

"If you tell me not to be afraid, I will not fear. If you insist that I believe, I will believe. Whatever you say."

If Jesus *is* a prophet, or perhaps more than a prophet, because He allowed Jairus to prostrate himself, then Jairus will cling to Jesus even more during this crucial time. What else can he do? vent his anger? cry out in despair? break up in sorrow? give up?

Jesus did not let anyone follow Him except Peter, James, and John. He knew the house would be full of family and friends grieving with the parents over the loss of this little girl. To take twelve more people inside would have been too much.

What in the world was Jesus going to do in Jairus's home? What in the world were they doing there with Him? What good could anyone possibly accomplish in this awful situation? Hopeless, that's what it was.

When they came to the home of the synagogue ruler, Jesus saw a commotion with people crying and wailing loudly.

Loud wailing—that's the way people from the Middle East react to death. Death is an ending, a disaster, a finality, and how can you do justice to your emotions unless you release your grief and sorrow?

> Jesus went in and said to them, "Why all this commotion and wailing? The child is not dead but asleep." But they laughed at him.

From crying to laughter with a snap of the fingers? How is that possible? Was their grief that shallow, only on the surface, loud and perhaps even offensive, but not soulful? Heartfelt anguish cannot turn from tears to laughter in the twinkling of an eye.

What is Jesus talking about? Is death a form of sleep from which we will awake in the next world? If so, why do we fear death? Every time we go to sleep, we wake up again. We know that from experience. Is that really what death is?

If it is true that we need not fear death, we must correct our erroneous ideas about it. We need to apply the words of Jesus right now! So it is not true that no one returns from the dead. So there is something behind that final curtain, even though we've not been allowed a peek?

> After Jesus put them all out, He took the child's father and mother and Peter, James, and John and went in where the child was. Jairus, still in shock, moved as if in a fog. He took the arm of his weeping wife, and they walked arm in arm into the room. They hardly knew what to expect. Jairus held on to Jesus' words. "Don't be afraid, just believe." Believe what? Believe now? He didn't know. He couldn't think clearly. As for the disciples, they,

too, wondered what they were doing there. They entered the house because they were told to, but they didn't know what might happen. Their eyes darted about, and they looked unsure.

The people waiting outside were offended. They talked in low whispers with each other. Why had Jesus taken charge? Who did He think He was? Why had He insisted on putting them outside?

"This is strange, isn't it?"

"Do you understand what's going on?"

"What is He doing in there? What authority does He have to tell us to remain here while He's in there?"

"Did you hear what He said? The girl is asleep!"

"That's crazy, isn't it? We saw her all stretched out on the bed with her eyes closed. She is gone. She is dead. She is not sleeping!"

But in the room, Jesus took the girl by the hand and said to her, "Little girl, I say to you, get up!"

The complete confidence of the human Jesus! This is not the Son of God in resurrection power, but the Son of Man, the human Jesus, who takes her cold hand and talks to her. His full assurance is in the God He knows intimately as His Father. The Father alone has power over death. God is life and therefore life will be triumphant. Death is a loser. If God is the Almighty, then life is victorious over death—always.

Jesus foreshadows His own resurrection by raising Jairus's daughter from the dead. From the beginning of His ministry, Jesus has complete trust in His future. He shared that belief with His disciples many times, foretelling the manner of His death and the certainty of His resurrection (on the third day). "Jesus, . . . for the joy set before him endured the cross, scorning its shame, and sat down at the right hand of the throne of God" (Hebrews 12:2). In His human existence, He lived by faith.

> And immediately the girl stood up and walked around. At this they were completely astonished.
>
> "Only God can raise the dead!"
>
> "If that is true, then what must we conclude about Jesus? If no one but God can bring the dead to life, then is Jesus *God?*"
>
> "Has God appeared on earth in human form?"
>
> "Is this the eternal God living among us, raising the dead, calmly assuring us that this little girl is not dead but only asleep?"

Is this what Jairus and his wife now believe? Do they accept Jesus' divinity, His claim of equality with God? And what of the people who waited outside—those who were critical and hostile before? How do they react when they see Daddy's girl alive again, walking out the front door of the house? They had seen her lifeless body stretched out on the bed. How can this be? They are amazed, reports the gospel of Mark. That amazement is a good description of faith, isn't it?

How will the world react when the graves are opened and the dead are raised? Will there be a kind of amazement? When we see Daddy's girl brought back from her ordeal, we can begin to trust Jesus with the future: "A time is coming when all who are in their graves will hear his voice, and come out—those who have done good, will rise to live, and those who have done evil, will rise to be condemned" (John 5:28).

Resurrection! The end of death's reign! The victory won! This is the good news that emerges from this story. Furthermore, the resurrection of Jesus trumpets other resurrections. He is the first to rise, which means that others will follow. The resurrection of Jesus destroys the arguments against eternal life. If Jesus has risen from the dead and is alive forevermore, the graves will be opened and the dead will be raised. The voice of the Son of God will awaken the dead. The dry bones will come to life. Because God is God, life—not death—will have the last word.

This is good news for all of us suffering, half-believing, wondering, questioning, irreverent sinners who tremble at the thought of death. We see that heavy, dark curtain of the night. We smell the foul odor of stench and decay. We despair because we cannot be sure of what lies beyond the awful abyss.

The only ray of light that pierces the thick curtain of death shines from the one who brought back Daddy's girl, who spoke with assurance and confidence about life, and who Himself came back from the abyss. "I am the Living One; I was dead and behold I

am alive forever and ever! And I hold the keys of
death and Hades" (Revelation 1:18).

> Jesus gave strict orders not to let any-
> one know about this and told them to give
> her something to eat.
> "Not talk about this? Is it possible to
> keep something like this under cover?
> That's impossible!"

Why does Jesus tell these people to remain silent?
Because if this story gets out people will flock to Him
from everywhere. So what is wrong with that? Isn't that
why Jesus entered the world, to bring in the kingdom of
God? The more the merrier, right? But if we turn to
Christ only for His miracles, only for what He can do
for us, the motive is unworthy. If we want Jesus only to
fulfill our needs, that is a selfish preoccupation, and
selfishness does not change our hearts. Our lives will
not be renewed. When our needs have been met, we will
go back to our old ways and say good-bye to Jesus.

We live in a consumer-oriented society. We want
our materialistic needs to be met, and our society knows
how to do that for us. But when our spiritual lives are
governed by the same cold hearts that direct our temporal lives, we will never please God. That is why Jesus
asks us to die to self, to take up our cross, to be willing
to sell everything. That is how we are to follow Him. We
cannot become disciples unless we commit to Him
wholeheartedly.

> With eyes wide open to the mercies of
> God, I beg you, my brothers [and sis-
> ters], as an act of intelligent worship,

> to give him your bodies, as a living sac-
> rifice, consecrated to him and accept-
> able by him. Don't let the world
> around you squeeze you into its own
> mould, but let God re-make you so
> that your whole attitude of mind is
> changed. Thus you will prove in prac-
> tice that the will of God is good, accept-
> able to him and perfect.
>
> —*Romans 12:1* PHILLIPS

Now you may get the impression from reading the Gospels that Jesus helps mostly the poor, the sick, the blind, the lame, the troubled outcasts of society. Even Jesus' disciples are ordinary, simple men who come from very ordinary vocations. But once in a while some-one "important" comes to Jesus. Jairus is a ruler of the synagogue, a respected elder who seeks Jesus in the daylight, not under the cover of darkness like the Phar-isee Nicodemus.

But assuming that Jairus serves on the board, where are the other elders? Why are they not seeking Jesus, too? Probably because they're not hurting. Life runs smooth for them. Life is good. The problem with those whom Jesus calls "the righteous" is that they feel no need for God. The lost sheep that has gone astray is found, but the ninety-nine in the fold who have untrou-bled lives do not believe they need Him.

Jesus has come not only for sinners, but also for people who seem to have it all together. They are nei-ther rich nor poor but belong to the solid middle class. They have enough material goods. They live well. They enjoy many events and types of entertainment.

But Daddy's little girl is very sick, and he can do nothing about it. Is your life troubled by something you cannot control? Is your teenager running with the wrong crowd? Are you afraid he may be on drugs? Have you tried to talk to her, but you get nowhere? Have you tried everything, but you can't reach him any more? Are you afraid of her mood swings, that she may even be suicidal? Do you live on the edge, fearful of what you may hear the next time the phone rings?

God gives most of us something we cannot handle. Maybe it's another person, some problem in our family. Maybe it's something in you. Some out-of-control situation caused the respected elder with a broken heart to seek Jesus. And Jesus will not only touch the body of Daddy's girl, He will also touch Daddy's and Mommy's hearts.

"He heals the brokenhearted and binds up their wounds," affirms the psalmist (Psalm 147:3). If your heart is broken, Jesus can bind up your wounds.

So thank God for that situation you cannot control! That one problem you cannot resolve will bring you to Jesus. Jesus can raise your son, your daughter, the one you are praying for. No one else can do this. No other philosophy or ideology will do, because Jesus alone is "the resurrection and the life." Jesus holds the power over death. He is the risen Lord. He has the keys of hades. He can lock and unlock.

That is why you, too, can fall at Jesus' feet to find salvation and eternal life!

> Then one of the synagogue rulers, named Jairus, came there. Seeing Jesus, he fell at his feet and pleaded earnestly with him "My little daughter is dying. Please come and put

your hands on her so that she will be healed and live." So Jesus went with him. . . .

While Jesus was still speaking [to a woman], some men came from the house of Jairus, the synagogue ruler. "Your daughter is dead," they said. "Why bother the teacher any more?"

Ignoring what they said, Jesus told the synagogue ruler, "Don't be afraid; just believe."

He did not let anyone follow him except Peter, James and John the brother of James. When they came to the home of the synagogue ruler, Jesus saw a commotion, with people crying and wailing loudly. He went in and said to them, "Why all this commotion and wailing? The child is not dead but asleep." But they laughed at him.

After he put them all out, he took the child's father and mother and the disciples who were with him, and went in where the child was. He took her by the hand and said to her, "Talitha koum!" (Which means, "Little girl, I say to you, get up!"). Immediately the girl stood up and walked around (she was twelve years old). At this they were completely astonished. He gave strict orders not to let anyone know about this, and told them to give her something to eat.

Mark 5:22

4

Blue Lady

A woman was there who had been subject to bleeding for twelve years—twelve years! The same physical problems for that long, flowing from one period to the next. She couldn't bear to think about it anymore. She had lost control over her body. That was the awful truth. She could do nothing about it—nothing. She had tried everything. She was desperate.

She had suffered a great deal under the care of many doctors, yet instead of getting better she grew worse. She had been to every doctor in town—every specialist recommended to her—an internist, a chiropractor, even a dietitian. Then she consulted a psychologist and a psychiatrist. She had been given tests, had been put on special medication, had received physical therapy, had tried acupuncture and different diets, but nothing stopped that bleeding—for twelve years!

She had spent all her money, too, all she had. Her medical insurance was canceled. She couldn't afford any more expenses. And what had she to show for it?

She was no better, only worse. She couldn't lead a normal life. She couldn't go where other people congregated, couldn't visit with friends. She even shunned most of her family. According to the law God had given to her people, she was unclean! In her condition she had to keep herself separate. She couldn't entertain or have people over. Maybe that was a blessing in disguise, because she felt so tired most of the time. She was exhausted. Nothing was worth the effort.

She lived in a perpetual state of depression. What if she had cancer? What a terrible thought! She lived in fear. It was easy to get upset about all of this. But what good did that do? Anger was no cure for her embarrassing situation. That's why she was blue, discouraged, moody, and disheartened. The clouds took away her sunny disposition. She used to be more carefree about life, a lot more fun. But that was twelve long years ago, and she could hardly remember those days now.

She had been married then. Life was good. They were a happy couple and the honeymoon had lasted at least two years. She became pregnant, and, except for a month of morning sickness, it was a wonderful and hopeful time. They were happily expectant. But something went wrong at the birth of the baby. She didn't know what. The baby was stillborn. The doctor couldn't explain it either. That was when the bleeding began. On further examination the doctor informed her that she would not be able to have any more children. Not ever. None of the doctors could provide her with a satisfactory explanation. And the bleeding never stopped.

That's when her husband left her. She couldn't blame him. He wanted children and she couldn't give him any. He had come from a large family. And Jewish wives were expected to bear sons. With all her physical problems, she couldn't be a mother, so she couldn't be a wife, either. Here she is, twelve years, later without a husband, without children. She longed for male companionship. But how could a man accept her? Not in her condition. Not now.

So this blue lady who had been subject to bleeding for so many years came up behind Jesus in the crowd and touched His cloak, because she thought, *If I just touch His clothes, I will be healed.*

After all these fruitless years, she had not yet given up hope! Remarkable! She had heard about Jesus, of course. His healings were widely reported, and wherever He ministered many people surrounded Him. She had no trouble locating Him, with the crowd pressing Him. She was about to take one last leap for the healing of her body. There was a chance, was there not? She had tried everything else, and although she couldn't help feeling bitter at times, the bitterness had not hardened her. Every other road had been closed, but she was willing to try one more time. The slightest glimmer of hope still flickered, even if she did have cancer. She was going to fight for her life, yes, even if it was cancer.

She wanted to touch Him, that was all, only to touch Him, nothing more—nothing less. He did not have to review her case. She did not want to recount all her symptoms to Him. She did not want to wait patiently in a doctor's office for another appointment, waiting to be seen, having to fill out all those forms, answering those terrible questions.

No more forms. No more waiting. No more embarrassment. All she wanted was one simple touch. He wouldn't even need to know. She just expected to get close enough to touch His clothes. That was all she desired—no pills, no medication, no injections, no needles, no treatments, no physical therapy, no special diet, no order for long-term rest—nothing else. Nothing more—only one touch.

One of her doctors asked, "What kind of belief is this? A shortcut to success? Are you trying to avoid the entire healing profession? circumvent the best hospital care in the county? dismiss all available scientific and medical assistance? the special care community? And what for?—for some healer who walks around without any credentials? He is not even an M.D.! For one touch of His clothing without His knowledge of what you are there for? Will that produce miracles? results? Isn't that rather extreme? unorthodox? Have you ever heard of anything as outrageous as this? Do you really believe it will do any good? Do you really think it will work?"

Is that all there is to it? One touch will heal you? One prayer and you receive an answer? Faith like a grain of mustard seed? Only believe? All things are possible, only believe?

A friend had warned her, "It seems to me you are wasting your time. Why don't you give it up? Just go away. It would be much better for you to return to your doctors again. They may have heard about something new. That's a better bet than this fly-by-night healer. Researchers are always using their creative minds to end fatal diseases, you know. It won't be long until they will have found a cure for cancer. And AIDS. It's bound to happen. Don't give up on the medical profession. Don't waste your time on a little touch of Jesus. That's far out—too far out. It's not going to work. Forget that!"

She thought, *If I just touch His clothes, I will be healed.* And she did! Immediately her bleeding stopped and she felt in her body that she was freed from her suffering.

Immediately! Only one touch! That was all. It worked! She was healed in her body and instantly she knew it, felt it. It was truly a miracle. His power flowed right through her fingers, up her arm and into her body like an electric current, producing a glorious healing. Years of suffering abruptly screeched to a halt and suddenly the agony was over. She was made whole, all because of that one little touch. It happened very quickly and very quietly. And no one would know. No one even suspected a thing. No more pills, no more treatments, no more fatigue, no more embarrassment, no more isolation, no more depression, no more feelings of worthlessness, no more self-criticism, no more self-rejection. What a relief to be actually and wonderfully healed!

It was like the story of Hannah of old. Hannah felt worthless because she was unable to have children. She was depressed because of her humiliation, and one day in her agitated state she entered the house of the Lord. She became excited in her prayers, and when the priest saw her, he thought she was drunk. She denied that. When the priest realized she was in earnest, he blessed her and prayed with her. She went home relieved of her anxiety, but, more than that, she believed the promises of God. She fully trusted that she would bring forth a son. She had no proof except for the witness in her soul. Before she became pregnant she believed her prayer had been answered by the Lord. She conceived and had a son. She named him Samuel and he became the first of Israel's prophets.

So, this woman struggling with the blues believed in one touch. She had endured such misery for twelve years, but it was wondrously finished. All of it! She decided that she would just leave quietly, go her way and not say a word to anyone. Her heart exploded with incredible joy, but on the outside no one could tell that anything had changed. She managed to conceal her feelings. Couldn't she just disappear without anyone knowing about this? She wouldn't have to tell Jesus about it, would she? He was so busy anyway. He was on His way to somebody's house where a little girl was seriously ill. That was more important. Jesus wouldn't care about her, would He?

At once Jesus realized that power had gone out from Him. He turned about in the crowd, and said, "Who touched my garments?"

He knew something had happened! He realized someone had touched Him and that it had made a difference. It was not just any old brushing by; it was a touch of faith, a pat from someone who was desperate, someone who had a great need, someone with hope. It wasn't just somebody who desired to get close to Jesus. There was intention in the touch, a desire to receive healing, to make a connection. And because this blue lady had made contact, believing, divine power was released! She had not lost her faith. Not then, not now.

"You see the people crowding against you," His disciples answered, "yet you ask, 'Who touched me?'" But Jesus kept looking around to see who had done it.

The disciples didn't have a clue. They were just minding their own business with all the people milling about. They had no information about anyone's healing. They didn't realize anything unusual had taken place. Everything seemed to be fine.

We may not have a clue either. We don't have any idea what Jesus accomplishes in someone's life—or when. We may even point to the wrong person in church, thinking someone has had an emotional experience because he or she looks so spiritual—whatever that means. But that may not be true at all. We have no idea who among us is touching the Lord, believing—who is really reaching out in faith. "God moves in a mysterious way His wonders to perform." Healing is not in our hands. How can we be sure when and where the power or the presence of God is experienced?

We're just innocent bystanders. Even now God may be saving someone, healing and transforming a life. Even now in this very moment when you pray in faith, the Lord can touch your body, mind, or spirit. And the rest of us remain in the dark. We haven't a clue because we don't know whom Jesus is touching, changing, saving, and healing. But we know that it can happen, just as it did to the blue lady.

She had disappeared into the crowd when she heard Him ask, "Who touched me?" And she couldn't very well remain silent. The woman, knowing what had happened to her, came and fell at His feet and, trembling with fear, told Him the whole truth.

She couldn't just walk away. She couldn't just ignore Him—not after this wonderful experience, not after this miracle that had changed her life. Jesus had not actually touched her physically, but she had touched Him. She fell down before Him. She humbled herself. She worshiped Him. She was overcome by His power, His kindness, His understanding, His mercy, His love.

She told Him everything—told Him her whole life in just a few moments, told Him what she had endured and how she had suffered for so long. She recounted everything, and He listened quietly, patiently, lovingly. But she realized He didn't really want to hear all the details nor did He have the time. He was, after all, on His way to another family where there was a great need. All He seemed to want of her was to trust the power of God for the heal-

ing of her body and her soul. And He
wanted her to live her life with that same
hope she had never lost, with that same
faith that had made her approach Him in
the first place. She must always live with
that kind of faith in God.

He motioned for her to stand up. He
said to her, "Daughter, your faith has
healed you. Go in peace, and be freed from
your suffering."

You are a daughter, a child of the covenant. You have a heavenly Father and
you belong in the family of God. Daughter,
your faith has healed you.

Faith is the key. Healing is wonderful, but faith is
more wonderful still. We would not be healed without
the faith that touches God. Peace is wonderful, but
faith is everything, since it is by faith that peace enters
the soul. By faith we receive salvation. Your faith has
sustained you for twelve long painful years. Your faith
is still active after all your trials and tribulations. Never
give up your faith in God, no matter what the circumstances. Life will be unbearably difficult at times, but
no matter how much you are tested, never stop trusting
in the living heavenly Father.

Where are you in your life now? Where are you after many years of hardship and failure? Where are you
after a long time of suffering and affliction? Where are
you after twelve years of misery? Do you still believe?
After twenty-two years? Thirty-three? How long can
you possibly endure your trials? How long can you live
with your shame, which you have not dared to share

with anyone? How can you cope any longer with your problems that you have patiently and dutifully carried? Can you make it through another day with that terrible hurt in your heart? Have you had it?

Are you discouraged? Do you feel ready to throw in the towel? Does it all seems so useless? Have you given up because nothing ever changes? Like the blue lady, you have tried everything and nothing works. Instead of getting better, things are only getting worse. Have you reached your limit?

Your temper is just too much. You've been told by people that you're out of control. When you get angry, you have to release it. So you just blow up. And now you're about to lose your family because of it. You can't keep hurting people around you with that explosive temper. You never could "stifle yourself," as Archie Bunker used to say on the old sitcom, *All in the Family*. You never could shut up and stay calm.

Or maybe you feel anger but you suppress it. You have been taught that you must never lose control, so all those feelings get shoved back inside. You stifle yourself very well, but inside of you there is a mixture of bad stuff. And that makes you depressed, makes you feel dejected because you can't really express what you feel. It is not true that all depression is caused by anger turned inward. There are other causes for what may be called "clinical depression." But some depression is caused by suppressed anger or by feelings of futility or resentment. Have you lived that way long enough?

Or is your head full of sex thoughts? You think sex all the time. You wonder whether other people are as obsessed with sex as you are. Sexual temptations get you into trouble again and again. You never could resist that kind of temptation. You were unable to control yourself in your teens, you didn't get much better in your twenties, and things aren't any different the older you become. You are one of those men who sees a good-looking woman walk down the street and you can get excited by just looking, as more than one man has confessed to me over the years. Oh, those secret thoughts, those sensual fantasies. How they trouble you since they're still being played out in your head after all these years!

And Jesus comes along. You hear about His healing power. You realize that He is understanding, compassionate, and caring. Maybe . . . well, maybe there is hope for you. You decide to take one last leap for your soul. It's a stretch of faith, but you reach out for the Savior. You want to touch Him, to connect, just as did that blue lady. Will it work? How can you be sure? But then, nothing else has helped and you have not changed. Those same old problems persist. You still indulge in that compulsive behavior. No one has broken your bad habits. And you've tried everything.

Like the blue lady, you too feel at a loss. Jesus is your only hope—not just anyone or anything—*Jesus*. She had heard good things about Him and that was enough to motivate her, but you and I know a lot more about Jesus than she ever did. She had heard about His miracles. She observed that Jesus was able to heal people. But that was about all she perceived. She didn't really know who He was or where He had come from.

You have heard the Christmas story. You know that God entered the world supernaturally when the angel Gabriel made that momentous announcement to a virgin. The child who was born was Immanuel, God with us. You know that He was called of God and baptized with the Holy Spirit. After overcoming the great temptation from Satan, in the wilderness, Jesus began His ministry. That is when you, like the blue lady, also heard about His healing miracles. But you have received more, the record of His teaching in the four gospels. You can read what Jesus taught. The words He spoke were from God.

You know more than His ministry; you have heard that Jesus came to offer His life as a ransom for us. You believe that Jesus died for our sins on the cross. As animals were sacrificed for the forgiveness of sins in the Old Testament, Jesus shed His blood to make atonement for our souls. The Lamb of God takes away the sin of the world. But death was not the end, because Jesus rose from the dead after three days. You have received witness of His resurrection and His numerous appearances to the disciples and others. You have heard of His ascension into the heavens, where He is exalted now at the right hand of the Father. You have also been informed that Jesus is the judge and coming king of the world. He will return in power and glory and bring in the kingdom of righteousness and peace, the kingdom of God. You know much more than the blue lady.

And do you think that the God of the universe cannot heal you from your affliction? cannot remove the problem from which you suffer? cannot touch and change you? You know a lot more than did this poor woman in the Gospels, so surely you can trust Him with your healing!

So come. Come now. Come to Jesus. He will allow you to make contact. You have nothing to fear. You need only believe. All things are possible. Only believe.

You are invited to come near enough to make contact, even in this crowd where many others are thronging Him. He will take notice of you. He will stop everything with everyone else and pay attention to you— only to you! That's true. You are just as special to Jesus as was this woman who came out of the blue. Just touch Him, believing, expecting. Not just any old touch will do.

I know you will come when you feel desperate enough, when you believe this is the only thing you can do! He is your last and only hope. The power is in Christ because it is the power of God. God will reach you even in your misery and shame, even with your discouragement, even in your helplessness—even if you have felt like a victim for ten, twenty, thirty, or more years.

For this is absolutely true: Jesus is here. He has saved, healed, forgiven, and transformed all who have come to Him through the ages. He has never rejected anyone. "All that the Father gives me will come to me, and whoever comes to me I will never drive away" (John 6:37)—never reject, never turn away, never cast out. Not then, not now.

Virtue flows out from God to you, virtue and salvation, forgiveness and mercy, healing and power—undeserved love for undeserving sinners. You are included; you are not excluded. Love and healing flow from almighty God—power for our powerlessness, acceptance for anyone abused or rejected. "Here is a trustworthy saying that deserves full acceptance: Christ Jesus came into the world to save sinners" (1 Timothy 1:15).

It is absolutely and wondrously true. Christ has come to save us. And that means Jesus brings not only the thrill of a conversion, but a lifetime of salvation. A conversion is wonderful. The initial realization of being forgiven and accepted is unforgettable. It is but a beginning. The salvation Jesus gives is not momentary but lasting. It is more than a marvelous experience—salvation is for life. Salvation is more than an initial miracle; it is an abiding reality.

"He who began a good work in you will carry it on to completion until the day of Jesus Christ" (Philippians 1:6). Salvation is for life!

"Daughter, your faith has healed you. Go in peace and be freed from your suffering." You are a daughter! You belong to the heavenly Father. You have come in faith. Live with that same faith.

A woman was there who had been subject to bleeding for twelve years. She had suffered a great deal under the care of many doctors and had spent all she had, yet instead of getting better she grew worse. When she heard about Jesus, she came up behind him in the crowd and touched his cloak, because she thought, "If I just touch his clothes, I will be healed." Immediately her bleeding stopped and she felt in her body that she was freed from her suffering.

At once Jesus realized that power had gone out from him. He turned around in the crowd and asked, "Who touched my clothes?"

"You see the people crowding around you," his disciples answered, "and yet you can ask, 'Who touched me?'"

But Jesus kept looking around to see who had done it. Then the woman, knowing what had happened to her, came and fell at his feet and, trembling with fear, told him the whole truth.

He said to her, "Daughter, your faith has healed you. Go in peace and be freed from your suffering."

Mark 5:25

5

A Powerless Nobody

A certain man—let's call him Joe—was paralyzed in the lower half of his body, so his mobility was severely restricted. He had lived his whole life with this physical limitation. Then Joe heard about the miraculous healings Jesus had performed, but he was not hopeful. He was very hesitant to approach Jesus because he did not expect any help. He had never walked. Ever. How could he hope for the healing of such a permanent condition?

Furthermore, many people with all kinds of maladies flocked to this prophet. Would Jesus of Nazareth even be concerned about him? Jesus may have had the power to heal people, but could he possibly heal *him*? He certainly did not want to bother the prophet. Even if Jesus did have the power, would he have any interest in his case? The problem was, of course, that he had no way of getting to Jesus, not in his condition. So the whole idea was preposterous.

He was sharing his thoughts with some friends, and as they were talking, his friends offered to take him to Jesus. He objected.

"No," Joe said, "that's too much trouble. I don't want you to put yourself out for me. It's not necessary."

"Not necessary? Of course it's necessary," they answered. "It will be no trouble. We'd like to be of help."

"No, I can't let you do this. I don't expect you to. It's too much to ask. Besides, you know how busy He is."

"How do you know that, Joe?"

"I just know. All those people. And I'm not worth it."

"Oh, don't be so humble," one of his friends replied. "of course you're worth it. You have suffered a lot. All your life. If you can be helped, we want to take you to Him."

Joe didn't argue anymore. He didn't want to tell his friends how embarrassed he was when they carried him around. He felt so ashamed of his weakness. He really didn't want to become a public spectacle, and that's what it was like to be transported by others. He felt ashamed of being ashamed, embarrassed about being embarrassed. He felt disgraced by his lower body, which he dragged around like a dead weight. People couldn't understand unless they had a similar infirmity.

When Jesus again entered Capernaum, the people heard that he had come
home. So many gathered that there was no
room left, not even outside the door, and
he preached the word to them.

The paralytic's friends insisted on
taking him in spite of his objections. So
what could he do? He consented. The four
of them lifted him and placed him on a pallet. They carried him to the home where
Jesus was reported to be.

They found Jesus teaching and minis-
tering, but they were not prepared for so
many people! People were swarming like
bees, everywhere. They had filled up the
house where Jesus was teaching. They
were even packed around the outside, listening to His words. What were the friends
to do?

Since they could not get him to Jesus
because of the crowd, the paralytic said:
"Let's just go back home. You can see it's
no use. It's impossible to get through this
crowd. He's busy. He's not interested in
me, anyhow. He doesn't even know I exist.
Let's not make a fuss. Let's just go home."

But his friends wouldn't hear of it.
"Look," they said, "we've come this far,
we're not giving up without a little effort.
We'll think of something. Just hold your
horses."

His friends tried to come up with a
plan that would work. If they couldn't get

through the crowd, they'd find another way. If they did not persist, Joe would have to return home in the same condition he had come. And that would only make him feel more defeated and dejected.

One of them suggested climbing up on the flat roof and making an opening to let Joe down into the living room. They lifted the helpless patient onto the roof and started to break up the mud-and-clay roof. The debris fell on the people below and on Jesus, too. Surprised and curious, they looked up, shielding their eyes from the falling debris, and saw glimmers of sunshine through the cracks.

When enough roofing had been removed, the four used ropes to lower the poor man on his pallet—like a crane transporting a heavy load into the hold of a cargo ship.

When Jesus saw their faith, He said to the paralytic, "My son, your sins are forgiven."

Jesus must have realized that the man who was suffering didn't have much faith. Perhaps some, but this whole weird happening was his friends' doing, after all. They had brought Joe here, they had broken up the roof, and they had lowered him at Jesus' feet. There the paralytic lay, preoccupied with his muddled thoughts, his feelings of shame and guilt and worthlessness. Yes, Jesus had hit the nail on the head. Joe was very aware of his sins. He certainly needed to be forgiven!

Joe's thoughts were a concern to him. It was not only his physical condition that bothered him. He was ashamed of his shortcomings, his weaknesses, his temptations. He was angry with his fate. He was miserable much of the time. He complained a lot, found fault with things, and even had bad thoughts about God. Why had God afflicted him like this? Why does God allow some people to suffer so much? Why did God single him out? Why was he overloaded with shame and guilt and weakness?

No, he certainly didn't want to be there on display in front of all these people and in front of Jesus, too. It was so humiliating. And his humiliation was not only physical because of his handicap, but spiritual, because Jesus had made a point of talking about his sins! Why had Jesus done this? The more Joe thought about it, the angrier he became. Yes, the sins of his mind and the sins of his heart were more serious than his physical condition. The physical disability was debilitating enough, but he had done great damage to his soul with his negative, rebellious, and often pessimistic spirit.

"Your sins are forgiven"? Joe had heard about the healing power of Jesus, but he had never been told that Jesus went around forgiving sins. No one had ever mentioned anything about forgiveness in connection with the physical miracles. So why did Jesus refer to his sins? Why did Jesus choose to make an example of him in front of all these people? Where did that come from at a time like this? Why didn't Jesus just concentrate on his affliction and heal him? That's what he was there for— not for his sinful nature.

Or was there some connection here? Were his sins *the cause* of his sickness? Or were his sins *the result* of his sickness? Was he sick because of his sins, or was it the reverse? There must be some connection or else Jesus would not have brought it up. But no, he could not be paralyzed because of his sins, because he had been disabled before he could sin. So, were his sins the result of his affliction? Probably. In some way. His thoughts were muddled, but then Jesus had actually announced his forgiveness! It was a word of pardon. "Your sins are forgiven." Forgiven? Really? Could it be true?

Now some teachers of the law were sitting there, thinking to themselves, "Why does this fellow Jesus talk like that? He's blaspheming! Who can forgive sins but God alone?"

Yes, it was blasphemy for any human being to claim to forgive sins. The Law of Moses clearly specified how people are to be forgiven: through the atonement and only the atonement. An animal had to be sacrificed and blood had to be shed. The blood covered the sin and that is why God can forgive sins. Only God can announce mercy and pardon, and God does so because of the atonement. How, then, can any human being—Jesus or anyone else— claim the prerogative of God?

These scribes were learned students of Holy Scripture. And they were right, of course. Forgiveness is God's business. It can never be a human achievement. So, who does Jesus think He is as He brashly announces the forgiveness of sins? Unless, of course—and this is the only possible conclusion we can reach—unless by this supreme announcement Jesus tells the paralytic and all who will listen that He has come from the Father with divine authority—that he is the Son of God! that He has the power to forgive sins and set people free! It's either that or blasphemy.

The scribes do not believe. They are not open to the possibility that Jesus has divine authority. They are the defenders of the historic position of the Jewish religion. They fully believe they are true to the eternal word of the Lord.

Immediately Jesus knew in His spirit what they were thinking in their hearts, and He said to them, "Why are you thinking these things? Which is easier: to say to the paralytic, 'Your sins are forgiven,' or to say, 'Get up, take your mat and walk'?"

The argument is solid. It is much easier to say, "Your sins are forgiven" than to ask the sick man to pick up his pallet and walk away. Why is it easier? Because speaking the words "your sins are forgiven" cannot be verified! How can anyone know that sins are forgiven? Who can be sure whether pardon has taken place? The words alone do not make it true. The grace of God is not a measurable commodity, nor is it a visible demonstration.

But to say "Get up, take your mat and walk" requires action. If the lame man fails to rise and walk, he has not been healed. That's obvious. If nothing happens to Joe there on the ground, it will prove how ineffective Jesus is.

Meanwhile, during this discussion Joe is still lying there in the hot house with the sun shining through the opening, sweating and feeling very uncomfortable. No one is paying much attention to him anymore. They have almost forgotten about him, since the scribes have had the spotlight turned on them. The paralytic stared up at the man from Galilee and waited.

"That you may know that the Son of Man has authority on earth to forgive sins. . . ." Jesus said to the paralytic, "I tell you, get up, take your mat and go home."

What? Get up? Right now? Actually rise to his feet? Is the prophet serious? How in the world can he possibly do that? Hold on a minute. In that split second Joe realized that if he picked up his pallet and walked away, he would be demonstrating that Jesus had the power of God to heal *and* to forgive sins. He realized that doing something visible would be a confirmation of experiencing something invisible—the forgiveness of sins. If he was able to walk, *he was at the same time a forgiven man!* That is why Jesus insisted that Joe *do* something, not merely *accept* something.

Did Jesus encourage him that if his body is healed, as momentous as that is, his soul will be made whole, as momentous as that can be? Can these happen simultaneously? Jesus did not ask Joe to pray. He did not insist that he repent or confess his sins. He did not even ask him to have faith, nor did Jesus make a fresh announcement of pardon. It had all been stated before. "Your sins are forgiven." Believe the naked truth. Believe the healing word. Believe the grace of God is for you— atonement for the soul!

But in order to receive the pardon of God, Joe had to get up and walk. That is what Jesus instructed him to do. He had never walked in his life. How could he just get up and stretch his weak, lame legs? He didn't think he would ever stand, since he had been lying down or sitting all his life. He *couldn't* stand up—or could he?

His friends, who had descended from the roof, positioned themselves around like guards on their perfectly healthy legs. They didn't offer any assistance. They watched Joe sit up on his pallet, but that was not unusual. Then he bent one leg at the knee and tucked it under him, and then the other leg. Now he made an effort to move forward, shifting his weight to his knees. He rested a moment before bringing his right foot forward. With his arm pushing down on his knee, he lifted himself slowly as his left foot moved in front of him. One of his friends reached out to steady Joe, but he shook him off.

"I can do it!" he grunted. "I can do it!" With those words he lifted himself and was standing for the first time in his life! He was as amazed as those who were watching him through this process. But there he stood. He bent over, picked up his pallet, rolled it up, put it under his arm, and took his first step. The crowd opened the way for Joe as slowly, carefully, deliberately he walked out of the house. His four friends followed behind him. The people just stared in amazement. "We have never seen anything like this!"

"Which is easier: to say to the paralytic, 'Your sins are forgiven,' or to say, 'Get up, take your mat and walk'? But

> that you may know that the Son of Man has
> authority on earth to forgive sins . . ."

Authority to forgive sins—that's what it is all about. That which only God can do in a human heart, Jesus can do. He is the Son of God, and He has the authority to forgive sins and to give eternal life to all who receive Him. And that is what the people were seeing with their eyes on that day in the house that needed its roof repaired—the healing of the body and the healing of the soul.

But how did Jesus know that this invalid needed more than a physical miracle? The need for forgiveness is universal. All have sinned and need the grace of God. Isn't that our condition too? No matter what our physical needs may be, we have this in common—we need atonement for our sins! And Jesus sees us dead in sins and trespasses. Jesus knows us. Jesus knows everything about us. Nothing escapes the Son of God.

When Philip invited his friend Nathanael to come and see Jesus, Nathanael was surprised that Jesus recognized him. "How do you know me?" Nathanael asked Jesus, since the two had not met before. "I saw you while you were under the fig tree before Philip called you." When Nathanael heard that, his response was, "Rabbi, you are the Son of God" (John 1:4). "I saw you," was enough to make Nathanael believe!

Jesus sees all of us. Do we want to be seen? Do we want to be known? We may hesitate because of the darkness within us. We feel so ashamed, so guilty, so unworthy. But if we answer, "Yes, I want to be seen," then we, too, will hear the words, "Your sins are forgiven." We are pardoned, and, believing the good news, life will be-

gin anew—even for those of us who took our fill of sinning. When we accept that we are seen, we will begin to
really see!

Oh, yes, the cure worked. There was no relapse.
The legs that had never walked before never gave out
again, not after that glorious healing. Jesus had received a powerless invalid, a person who felt unworthy
and unacceptable for such a long time, but none of the
damage and none of those bad feelings returned, and
that was a relief. He had been healed, touched, and
changed. And the change was complete. He walked
freely, and his spirit was released from prison.

Not that the healing made him perfect—of course
not. But with the forgiveness of sins came renewal. It
always does. The grace of God does a creative work in
our souls. We are no longer so negative, so hard on
ourselves. We do not continue to condemn ourselves,
nor do we consider ourselves worthless. Where we
thought we were of little value before, we now realize
that we are of value to God because of the Atonement.
Christ died for our sins, and that means Jesus cared
enough to give His life for us. We are cared for. We are
loved by God.

Yes, the former paralytic stopped being so critical,
so negative, so pessimistic. He saw God in a new light.
God had healed him, forgiven him, pardoned him. He
was the recipient of two miracles—a miracle in his body
and a miracle in his soul. And the greater of the two was
the second, for Jesus made Joe feel loved and accepted.
Jesus brought him peace and freedom.

There is a relationship between sin and sickness—
not that either can cause the other—not that. My sins
cannot make me ill, any more than my illness can cause

me to be more sinful. And yet each can exert an influence on the other. When I become sick, I become more negative and despondent. The longer my illness persists, the worse I feel, and the greater is my tendency to lose hope. My disease does not automatically make me turn to God. Instead I often feel despondent, listless, yes—rotten. I certainly don't put my best foot forward when I've got it in a cast.

It is equally true that my sins can increase physical ills. A thousand years before Christ, David insightfully wrote about the effect of sin on sickness: "When I kept silent [about my sin], my bones wasted away through my groaning all day long" (Psalm 32:3). The thought that sins can cause sickness is not new! When I hide my sins and refuse to make confession, my body picks up this bad attitude. It is almost as if my stubbornness enters the bloodstream and is transported through my whole being. As a result my bodily functions don't work normally. My unconfessed sin can make me tired and cranky and difficult to live with.

And just as there is a relationship between sickness and sin, so a similar relationship exists in the healing process. For one thing, we are saved by faith: "Since we have been justified through faith, we have peace with God through our Lord Jesus Christ" (Romans 5:1). Salvation is the gift of God. By faith we accept the grace of God, which is freely offered us in Christ. And we are justified.

We are also healed by faith. "Your faith has made you whole" is often the affirmation of Jesus to those who are being healed. Healing takes place not only through medicine and treatment, which will indeed benefit, but also through faith. You need to believe that you will become well. Faith is instrumental in both cases. Faith saves your body and your soul.

In Psalm 103:3, David brings the two together. Just as he first observed the connection between sin and sickness in Psalm 32 ("When I kept silent, my bones wasted away"), he further unites the two in the healing process: "[The LORD] forgives all your sins and heals all your diseases." God heals and forgives, by faith. So, this powerless weakling walked away and was forgiven at the same time. The physical and the spiritual miracles are intertwined. The whole person has been saved!

This does not always happen, of course. But it can happen. I remember a woman in her thirties, a mother of two, who talked with me about her anger at her husband, at life, at God. She also suffered from severe and persistent physical symptoms. When she confessed and made a new commitment to Christ, she was able to stop being angry toward both God and her husband. A week later she reported that at the time she made her commitment, her stomach pains and other abdominal troubles completely disappeared. And those problems never returned. Her spiritual and physical transformation happened at the same time.

I have observed such changes in others when they received the forgiveness of sins—changes that produce spiritual life, mental stability, and physical well-being. We are unified beings. "May your whole spirit, soul and body be kept blameless [until] the coming of our Lord Jesus Christ" (1 Thessalonians 5:23). Salvation is for the whole person.

How often the saving presence of God leads to a healthier life! Headaches are gone. Nausea is gone.

Nerves are no longer frayed. Physical ailments are cured. This paralytic walked away with his bedroll under his arm, and that bedroll carried a lot of negative debris. He had been set free by the Savior: "Son, your sins are forgiven."

No, it doesn't always happen like that. But sometimes it does. And while a physical healing has only temporal consequences, the salvation of the soul is eternal.

> When Jesus again entered Capernaum, the people heard that he had come home. So many gathered that there was no room left, not even outside the door, and he preached the word to them. Some men came, bringing to him a paralytic, carried by four of them. Since they could not get him to Jesus because of the crowd, they made an opening in the roof above Jesus and, after digging through it, lowered the mat the paralyzed man was lying on. When Jesus saw their faith, he said to the paralytic, "Son, your sins are forgiven."
>
> Now some teachers of the law were sitting there, thinking to themselves, "Why does this fellow talk like that? He's blaspheming! Who can forgive sins but God alone?"
>
> Immediately Jesus knew in his spirit that this was what they were thinking in their hearts, and he said to them, "Why are you thinking these things? Which is easier: to say to the paralytic, 'Your sins are forgiven,' or to say, 'Get up, take your mat and walk'? But that you may know that the Son of Man has authority on earth to forgive sins . . . ." He said to the paralytic, "I tell you, get up, take your mat and go home." He got up, took his

mat and walked out in full view of them all.
This amazed everyone and they praised God,
saying, "We have never seen anything like
this!"

Mark 2:1

"Old Nick"

It is an honor to be chosen as an elder in Israel. I don't know why I deserved such an honor. I don't know why I was elected a member of the Sanhedrin. There are, after all, only seventy of us in this exclusive body!

You see, I'm not a holy individual. I am not more holy than anyone else. I am an ordinary person, a very ordinary man. My election came as a complete surprise. I didn't apply for the position, you understand. I was chosen by majority vote when I was in my fifties. I thought becoming a member of the Sanhedrin would give me a certain amount of confidence. You may as well know that self-confidence has always been a problem for me. I don't know why. I believe in God. That's not a problem. But I don't know if I *really* believe in God. Do you know what I mean? I pray, but I don't know if my prayers are heard. I don't get answers to my prayers. I don't know that God cares about me. You see, I am very good at asking questions, but I don't find many answers.

So, I thought that becoming a member of the Sanhedrin would give me more confidence. I took my position seriously. But religion can be a kind of business. You get put on committees, you attend many meetings, you vote. That does not make you spiritual. I did not gain self-confidence. Religion can be more of a business than a spiritual experience. Until—but let me tell you about that.

I was in my sixties (that sounds a little better than admitting I was actually sixty-seven) when we first received reports about Jesus. He was from a small village in Galilee. He was the son of a carpenter, uneducated, yet He managed to attract crowds. They claimed that He was able to heal people—could perform miracles. My colleagues tended to be cynical about Him. I was not sure, but they said that His work took place among simple people, highly suggestible country folk. And everybody knows that they will believe anything.

The first time Jesus came to Jerusalem, my colleagues decided to ignore Him. They insisted that we avoid Him, too. If we were seen near Jesus, we would be censured by the Sanhedrin—maybe lose our jobs! That was the official policy, but I kept my ear to the ground. And what I heard interested me greatly. His teaching had a ring of truth to it. He spoke about the kingdom of God, about love and purity, humility, redemption, righteousness, and faith. And people in Jerusalem reported a few healings.

I decided that I wanted to see Him. But how could I talk with Him without being observed? I couldn't approach Him in broad daylight. Perhaps at night? Under the cover of darkness? I found out where Jesus was living. I took off my official robes, put on some simple clothes, and went to the house where He was staying. I was brought into a small living room and given a private audience.

Jesus walked in. He wore a plain robe. He was an ordinary-looking man. Quite young. About thirty, I would guess—not even half my age. About my height, a slimmer waistline than mine! And I saw at once that there was something about Him that I didn't have—self-confidence! I sensed it in the way He stood—in His bearing, in His eyes, and, later of course, in the way He talked. He motioned for me to sit down.

After introducing myself as one of the seventy (I wanted Him to know that), I said: "Sir, thank you for allowing me this private interview. I did not come to you in the daytime, because I didn't want any of my friends to see me with you. You probably realize that the Sanhedrin are not friendly toward you. They do not like you here in Jerusalem, and they do not like you in Galilee, for that matter. They don't believe that you are anyone special. They don't believe in what you call 'signs,' and they don't value your teaching either." I took a deep breath.

"But I don't share those sentiments. I have listened to reports of your works and your words, and I believe that you must be a man of God. You have come to us from the Lord God of Abraham, Isaac, and Jacob. No one can do the miracles that you are doing without the blessing of God. That much I believe. Sir, you must be a prophet from God, and I would like to ask you about the kingdom of God. What is this kingdom of God you talk about?"

He looked at me with His dark, piercing eyes. He didn't say anything for a moment. And then His words shook me to the foundation of my being.

"Nicodemus," Jesus said, "Listen to what I'm going to say to you. It is truth, eternal truth you are about to hear. *No one can see the kingdom of God who is not born again.*"

I was dumbfounded. "Born again?" I asked. "What do you mean by that? I don't understand. I ask you about the kingdom of God, and you respond that I must go through a birth process? Jews do not believe in reincarnation. You are not talking about reincarnation, are you? No, I didn't think so. How can I be born again at my age? or at any age? How can I return to my mother's womb? Besides, my mother is dead, so that's impossible. And what has this to do with God? I ask you about the kingdom of God, and you tell me this? What are you talking about?"

"Nicodemus," He replied, "I do not mean a physical birth. Certainly not. And I am not talking about reincarnation either. I mean a spiritual birth. There is a natural birth and there is a spiritual birth. There is a natural beginning to life and there is a spiritual beginning. Do you understand that? That which is born of flesh is fleshly, and that which is born of the Spirit is spiritual. Listen to the truth, Nicodemus. You have already been born physically. We all have. Have you been born spiritually?"

"No, I have not," I replied. But I was thinking about my lack of self-confidence and my pressing questions about God.

"Don't be surprised at what I am telling you, then. It is a fundamental truth. You must be spiritually reborn, born from above, born of God."

He must have seen my quizzical expression. I really didn't understand Him. As I told you, I can ask questions. I don't have many answers. What was this strange new teaching?

"Let me explain this to you, Nicodemus," He continued. "You know when the wind is blowing, don't you? You can feel it.

Sometimes you hear it. But you don't know where it's coming from, do you? Oh, yes, you point to the west and you say it's an ocean breeze. We will have a cool day. But where does the wind come from? And where is it going? To the east, the desert? Yes, but how far? Where does it end? Or does it?

"What I am telling you is that there is a mystery about wind. Have you not read in the Scriptures that God causes the wind to blow and the waters to flow? So it is with everyone who is born of God. In the same way that God causes the wind to blow, God shows his word to Jacob and his commandments to Israel. You will find this in the Psalms. This is a great mystery, but you will believe when the Spirit of God enters your spirit. You will know it, like the wind."

I understood His illustration, but the reference in Psalms was obscure. I had probably read it sometime, but I had forgotten. Besides, there is nothing about new birth in the writings of Moses or the prophets.

"How can this be?" I asked. "How am I to be born anew?"

He looked at me again with those deep, dark eyes.

"I'm really surprised," He said slowly. "You are a teacher in Israel. You are one of the select seventy. You are a student of the Word of God. You know the teaching of Moses and of the Prophets. You are a scholar, and you don't know what I'm talking about? Don't you realize that all the great heroes of faith—Abraham, Isaac, Jacob, Moses, Joshua, Samuel, David, Solomon, the prophets—all of them were born anew? They did not all have the same experiences. Abraham heard a voice and left his country, Jacob wrestled with an angel, Moses listened to God at a burning bush. They all had spiritual experiences. They were all born from above. And you want me to explain to you how this happens?"

I waited for Him to continue.

"This spiritual birth is of God. I have talked with you about earthly things, and you don't grasp it. If you cannot understand what takes place here, how can I explain to you the heavenly process? But believe me, you must be born anew, born of God."

I wanted to ask Him more about the kingdom of God, the miracles, and the signs, but I sensed that He was not willing to discuss anything else. What He had told me was essential for me for now. We were standing up to say good-bye, but before I left He added something else.

"Nicodemus, I will give you a clue about this new birth. Do you remember the story of our people in the desert when there was a plague of poisonous snakes? The Israelites were attacked, bitten by snakes, and they were dying. Then Moses was instructed by the Lord to put a brass snake on a wooden pole. All those who had been poisoned who looked on that snake were healed. Well, as Moses lifted up a serpent in the wilderness, so must the Son of Man be lifted up! Whoever looks on the Son of Man will be born again, will not perish, but will have eternal life."

I had trouble understanding this also. Oh, I remembered the illustration from Moses. That's a familiar story. But why did Jesus bring up that ghastly example? Why did He compare Himself to a brass snake in the desert? Lifted up on a pole? For what reason?

Only later did I realize the importance of those words.

Two years went by. Jesus returned to Galilee, and my business kept me in Jerusalem—committees and meetings and voting on policy. I never did have another private conversation with Him, but when He visited Jerusalem for the Feast of Tabernacles two years later, I was in the crowd. By this time He was the topic of many conversations. And members of the Sanhedrin were allowed to hear Him. They intended to argue with Him and make Him look bad in front of the people.

When He arrived here, He went directly to the temple grounds. Many of us heard Him there. Other elders came to criticize; I came to listen. On the final day of the feast Jesus made an announcement: "If any of you is thirsty, come to me and drink." This produced an immediate reaction.

"Are you the prophet who should come?" some people shouted when they heard this. "Or are you the Messiah we are looking for? Which? Who are you?"

During this commotion one of our elders quieted the crowd.

"Listen to me, people," cried the elder. "I am one of the seventy, one of the Sanhedrin. I tell you that no prophet will arise out of Galilee. The Messiah cannot appear in Galilee. The Holy Scriptures teach that the Messiah comes from the line of King David. He is to be born in Bethlehem. Read it in the prophet Micah. And Bethlehem is not in Galilee, but right here in Judea, just south of Jerusalem."

Later I learned that the elder had been sent by Caiaphas, our executive officer of the Sanhedrin. I also discovered that Caiaphas had given orders to the temple police to arrest Jesus. Then Caiaphas called a meeting of the Sanhedrin. He expected the police to bring Jesus so that he would have the man in his power. That's when I first heard about the plot.

I need to tell you a little about Caiaphas, our president. He was a religious man, of course. I would say he was religious on the outside. On the inside it was a different matter. He was controlling, shrewd, greedy, self-centered. He was a man of power. He determined policy and carried it out. He was, in the words of Jesus, like a white tomb—painted white on the outside, but inside full of decaying bones and death.

We had no sooner assembled when the police officers returned—empty-handed. Caiaphas fully expected them to have seized Jesus, but no.

"Why didn't you bring Him?" Caiaphas asked the sergeant.

"Sir," answered the sergeant, "We couldn't. The people were all around Him. They hung on every word. Some believed Him to be the Prophet. We couldn't arrest Him. And besides this, while we were listening to His teaching, we, too, were impressed by what He said. He is unusual, Sir. I tell you, we've never heard anyone speak like that man."

"Have you lost your mind or are you just plain stupid?" roared Caiaphas. "How do you know no one ever spoke that way? Are you crazy? Do you see any of us believing this impostor? Don't you think we will know the Messiah when He comes? We are the scholars. We know the Law and the Prophets. We study the Holy Scriptures. As for those people flocking to Him, they don't know anything. They are stupid and ignorant. They do not read the Bible. They do not know what the Holy Book says. I tell you they are cursed. They know nothing about religious matters, and you listen to them?"

He stood there getting red in the face.

"I should think that when we give you orders to arrest this deceiver, that you would follow our orders. Who are you to take such important issues into your own hands? You are the police and you don't know anything about spiritual things. We will dismiss you now, but the next time, you will bring Him to us."

The police excused themselves and left quietly. Caiaphas sat down. A deathly silence fell over the assembly. I couldn't take it any longer. I realized that I had to do something. My conscience would not allow me to remain passive.

"Caiaphas," I said, rising to my feet, "May I raise a point of order?"

"Of course, Nicodemus," he said, somewhat condescendingly, I thought. He was probably wondering why I wanted to speak.

"Your honor, does our law judge anyone before it hears him? Can we pass judgment on this man without giving Him a hearing? without questioning Him?"

He sneered at me. "Nicodemus," he spit out my name—Caiaphas can be humiliating and cruel, devastating. "Nicodemus, what's with you? Are you from Galilee?" He laughed at his own joke. "No. You're not! Don't you know the Scriptures? No prophet arises from Galilee. Right? You ought to know that, too. Go back and read your Bible, and you will see this whole Galilee stupidity is a deception. We certainly don't need any examination of this false prophet."

I was glad I had spoken, even though it didn't do any good. Caiaphas was not through. "And mark my words. It is better for us to get rid of this Galilean than it would be for us to lose our position in Israel. We will need to take action against Him, soon." The course was set for the Sanhedrin.

One final time Jesus came to Jerusalem. It was to be His last. For a few days He was seen around town and He spoke in the temple, but then He was betrayed by one of His own. Caiaphas learned His whereabouts and sent the police to arrest Him. They cornered Him in Gethsemane and brought Him to Caiaphas. It was in the middle of the night!

Caiaphas called a meeting that very night. It was an impossible time for a meeting—after midnight—but he would not wait. He had Jesus in his power, and he

was not about to let Him get away. By the
time word reached me, it was all but over.
I did get there for what proved to be the fi-
nale. I understand that Jesus refused to
answer any of the accusations against Him,
and when I arrived Jesus was standing
with His hands tied behind His back, His
head slightly bowed, with two policemen
on either side.

"Jesus of Nazareth," growled Caiaphas, "You say you are a man of God.
You believe in the law of God. I am about
to put you under that law. You are aware
of the fact that you must answer under
oath or else you will be defying the law of
God."

Every Jew was aware of that. Not to
answer under oath was an insult to God
and to the commandments. Not to answer
was the same as admitting your guilt. You
would be considered a bad Jew.

Caiaphas spoke slowly, deliberately:
"Jesus, I charge you before the living God
to answer under oath. Tell us, are you the
Messiah, the Son of God?"

I heard His answer myself. "I am! And
I tell you this, the next time you see me I
will be seated at the right hand of the Almighty and coming on the clouds of heav-
en."

That was all it took.

"Blasphemy!" cried Caiaphas. He
tore his robes in the traditional gesture of

repentance. He wanted to show his disgust. "Utter blasphemy! You have heard it. We have only one course open to us now. This man is guilty and is worthy of death!"

"Guilty," cried the Sanhedrin, and many tore their robes. I did not.

Jesus was immediately taken to Pontius Pilate, the Roman official. We Jews did not have the power to carry out the sentence. Only Rome could enforce the penalty of death. Pilate examined Him, but when he learned Jesus was from Galilee, he sent Him to King Herod. Herod governed in Galilee under the Romans. Herod, unable to get a word out of Him, mocked Him, and soon returned Him to Pilate.

By this time Caiaphas had changed the charge! He never mentioned the blasphemy or the question of the Messiah to Pilate. The Romans didn't care about religious issues, so Caiaphas informed Pilate that Jesus claimed to be a king. He knew that Rome would not tolerate a king in competition with Caesar.

Frankly, I don't think Pilate was ever convinced of Jesus' guilt. He punished Jesus, had Him beaten, flogged, and crowned with thorns, but Pilate wasn't altogether sure he had a king on his hands—at least not a dangerous one. Nevertheless, their conversation ended when Jesus was

convicted. The Roman washed his hands
of the whole business—refused to accept
responsibility for his verdict—and sen-
tenced Jesus to die.

I went out to the hill to see the sorry
death, the body lifted up on that wooden
monstrosity, hanging between two condemned criminals. And as I saw Jesus on
the cross, His words came back to me.
"As Moses lifted up the snake in the
desert, so the Son of Man must be lifted
up." So that is what He was talking
about! The manner of His own death!
And how were the Israelites healed? by
looking on that snake, by believing. If
anyone, if I, looked on that cross and believed, then I would be born again, then I
would receive eternal life.

I stood there for a long time full of my
thoughts. I remembered His words before
the Sanhedrin. He is the Son of God! He
will come again at the right hand of the Almighty! And now the Messiah hangs on a
cross rejected, despised, forsaken. He is,
as another prophet has said, the Lamb of
God who takes away the sin of the world—
the sacrifice for our sins. For us. For me.

I can't describe exactly what happened as I stood meditating and praying,
but something happened to old Nick at the
cross—a spiritual experience. I was born
again, born from above. Just as I feel the
wind, I know the Spirit entered my soul.

I was so moved that I didn't hear another member of the Sanhedrin slip up beside me. "I thought I might find you here," he said.

I turned around. "Joseph?" I asked. "What are you doing here?"

"Do you remember the day you spoke up at our meeting and asked for a point of order? You said that we should hear a man before we condemn him?"

How could I forget? "Of course I remember," I said.

"Well, ever since that day I realized that you were drawn to Jesus, just as I have been."

I clasped his hand. We stood shoulder to shoulder in silence. By midafternoon the Sanhedrin had already arranged for the crucified to die before sundown. Caiaphas did not want the bodies to remain on the crosses for the Sabbath. He requested Pilate to send Roman soldiers to the hill to break the legs of the condemned. You understand, don't you, that when they break the legs, the crucified can no longer lift themselves up to draw breath and, not being able to get air, will die quickly of asphyxiation.

Pilate, grumpy and out of sorts, agreed to it. We saw the soldiers arrive at the crosses. They broke the legs of one of the thieves, but Jesus' head was already bowed. They wanted to make sure He was not faking death. A soldier pierced His side. The body was lifeless. Jesus was dead.

"Come on," Joseph said, "Let us go to Pontius Pilate."

"Why?" I asked.

"I have a tomb—a new tomb. I want to take the body of Jesus down from the cross and give Him a decent burial."

"Yes," I said. "I'm with you."

Pilate gave us an audience, but he didn't believe that Jesus was dead already. He insisted on calling the centurion. After the centurion verified the death, Pilate granted us permission to take down the body.

On our way to the hill we bought some spices, aloes, and myrrh to anoint the body, and also some linens. We took down the mangled body and wrapped it in the spices and linens, laying Him in the tomb before nightfall, before the Sabbath started. His mother, a disciple, and a couple of women helped us. We had done what we could.

The first time I saw Jesus I came by night. The last time it was in broad daylight.

The first time I was fearful and afraid. The last time I was changed, even confident. I've always had trouble with self-confidence, but something happened to me at the cross of Jesus. Being born anew gave me confidence. Now I know God cares about me!

I realized, of course, what my new commitment would mean! By my identification with Jesus, courageous or not, I moved myself out of the Sanhedrin. I sealed my fate as a member of the select seventy. I lost my job and, with it, the respect I had gained during my tenure. I sacrificed everything. But it was well worth it. I had to do it. I have to respect myself, and my life has taken on new meaning!

I believe God. Now I really believe God!

What a bad time for me to emerge from the shadows. Jesus is dead, and now I declare myself a believer? not during His ministry, but after it's all over? Instead of becoming a disciple of the living Jesus, I announce that I am a follower when He is dead? That is poor timing! Or is it?

Well, you know what happened next. Jesus didn't remain in Joseph's tomb. He came forth—miraculously. He arose from the dead and appeared alive to the disciples—made many appearances. I didn't see Him, but I didn't need to. I believe the reports. He is the Son of God.

When Jesus ascended into heaven to the right hand of God, I believed that too. It was exactly as He had predicted to the Sanhedrin. After all, I had heard Him myself!

John, who had been at the cross when we took down the body, introduced me to the disciples. At first they were skeptical, but I told them of my conversion. My life took on new meaning. I experienced joy and peace. I can't tell you how incredible it has been. A spiritual birth will change your life! It did mine—even so late in years. But, it's never too late—not for anyone. Not for you, not for me. Never too late.

It is as Jesus said—when you are spiritually born, *you will see the kingdom of God.*

Now there was a man of the Pharisees named Nicodemus, a member of the Jewish ruling council. He came to Jesus at night and said, "Rabbi, we know you are a teacher who has come from God. For no one could perform the miraculous signs you are doing if God were not with him."

In reply Jesus declared, "I tell you the truth, no one can see the kingdom of God unless he is born again."

"How can a man be born when he is old?" Nicodemus asked. "Surely he cannot enter a second time into his mother's womb to be born!"

Jesus answered, "I tell you the truth, no one can enter the kingdom of God unless he is born of water and the Spirit. Flesh gives birth to flesh, but the Spirit gives birth to spirit. You should not be surprised at my saying, 'You must be born again.' The wind blows wherever it pleases. You hear its sound, but you cannot tell where it comes from or where it is going. So it is with everyone born of the Spirit."

"How can this be?" Nicodemus asked.

"You are Israel's teacher," said Jesus, "And do you not understand these things? I tell you the truth, we speak of what we know, and we testify to what we have seen, but still you people do not accept our testimony. I have spoken to you of earthly things and you do not believe; how then will you believe if I speak of heavenly things? No one has ever gone into heaven except the one who came from heaven—the Son of Man. Just as Moses lifted up the snake in the desert, so the Son of Man must be lifted up, that everyone who believes in him may have eternal life."

John 3:115

Many in the crowd put their faith in him. They said, "When the Christ comes, will he do more miraculous signs than this man?" The Pharisees heard the crowd whispering such things about him. Then the chief priests and the Pharisees sent temple guards to arrest him.

On the last and greatest day of the Feast, Jesus stood and said in a loud voice, "If anyone is thirsty, let him come to me and drink. . . ."

On hearing his words, some of the people said, "Surely this man is the Prophet."

Others said, "He is the Christ."

Still others asked, "How can the Christ come from Galilee? . . ."

Finally the temple guards went back to the chief priests and Pharisees, who asked them, "Why didn't you bring him in?"

"No one ever spoke the way this man does," the guards declared.

"You mean he has deceived you also?" the Pharisees retorted. "Has any of the rulers or of the Pharisees believed in him? No! But this mob that knows nothing of the law—there is a curse on them."

Nicodemus, who had gone to Jesus earlier and who was one of their own number, asked, "Does our law condemn anyone without first hearing him to find out what he is doing?"

They replied, "Are you from Galilee, too? Look into it, and you will find that a prophet does not come out of Galilee."

John 7:31

Those who had arrested Jesus took him to Caiaphas, the high priest, where the teachers of the law and the elders had assembled. . . .

The chief priests and the whole Sanhedrin were looking for false evidence against Jesus so that they could put him to death. But they did not find any, though many false witnesses came forward . . . . Jesus remained silent.

The high priest said to him, "I charge you under oath by the living God: Tell us if you are the Christ, the Son of God."

"Yes, it is as you say," Jesus replied. "But I say to all of you: In the future you will see the Son of Man sitting at the right hand of the Mighty One and coming on the clouds of heaven."

When the high priest tore his clothes and said, "He has spoken blasphemy! Why do we need any more witnesses? Look, now you have heard the blasphemy. What do you think?"

"He is worthy of death," they answered.

Matthew 26:57, 59

Later, Joseph of Arimathea asked Pilate for the body of Jesus. Now Joseph was a disciple of Jesus, but secretly because he feared the Jews. With Pilate's permission, he came and took the body away. He was accompanied by Nicodemus, the man who earlier had visited Jesus at night. Nicodemus brought a mixture of myrrh and aloes, about seventy-five pounds. Taking Jesus' body, the two of them wrapped it, with the spices, in strips of linen. This was in accordance with Jewish burial customs. At the place where Jesus was crucified, there was a garden, and in the garden a new tomb, in which no one had ever been laid. Because it was the Jewish day of Preparation and since the tomb was nearby, they laid Jesus there.

John 19:38

7

Five Weddings and No Funerals

It was another hot and humid day in the Holy Land. The sun rose to the middle of the sky, announcing the most intense, sweltering time of day. She had been up for only a couple of hours, having slept in after a playful night. She dressed herself, had some cereal and fruit, read the morning paper, and then went out to fetch water. She always took this walk in the middle of the day to avoid the other women, who went in the cool of the early morning. They didn't like her; she didn't like them, either. It had been like this for some years.

No, it wasn't that she was lazy or anything. She just avoided them so she could be left alone with her thoughts. No one was outside at that impossible noon hour. It was too hot. She didn't mind the heat that much. She was used to it by now. As she made her way to the well, she saw a man sitting there. Her first reaction was annoyance. What was He doing there? She'd wanted to be alone. She'd looked forward to a chance to meditate, a quiet time to think about God. And He would interfere simply because He was there, invading her privacy.

It was too late to do anything about it now. She was almost at the well, and coming closer she realized the man was a Jew. She could tell by His clothing, His beard. Breathing a sigh of relief, she realized He would be no problem after all, because Jews don't associate with Samaritans. They want nothing to do with them. They look down on Samaritans simply because Samaritans are not really Jews. They are descendants of mixed marriages. Today she didn't mind that so much, because now He would leave her alone! He wouldn't start a conversation, wouldn't even say hello. And that was just fine with her.

When the woman came to draw water, Jesus said to her, "Will you give me a drink?"

She was shocked. She was too stunned to reply. Her voice choked and she couldn't even ask, "Are you talking to me?" Nothing came out of her mouth. Why was He asking her for water? Why did He start a conversation? It was unorthodox, unheard of. What was He thinking? What did He really want? Did He have some other motive? Then she got her voice back.

She said to him, "You are a Jew and I am a Samaritan woman. How can you ask me for a drink?"

I don't deal with people like you, she implied, and you look down on people like me. I know that. We're so much dirt to you. So, what are you doing asking me for a drink? That is what she was thinking.

Jesus had three strikes against Him. He was a Jew and she was a Samaritan. He was a man and she was a woman. Jews don't talk to Samaritans, men don't talk to women, and Jewish men certainly don't respect Samaritan women. And furthermore, Jews and Samaritans don't drink out of the same cups! So how could He be so coarse as to ask for a drink when He didn't even have a cup from which to drink? He would have to use hers, and that was not acceptable.

What was He after? Did He really want a drink, or was He looking for something else? What did He take her to be? Men—they only think of one thing. She was beginning to feel uncomfortable.

Jesus answered her, "If you knew the gift of God and who it is that asks you for a drink, you would have asked me and I would have given you living water."

What in the world did He mean by that? What was He talking about? Water is water. What else could be water? What is "living water" supposed to mean? And what is this special gift of God? God gives us everything. God is the Creator of heaven and earth. God creates the sun and the moon and the mountains and the trees and the water. God is the giver of all things, the giver of life itself. What was He talking about? What is this special gift of God?

What is this living water? What could He give her that she couldn't get right here out of the well? Who was this man who said such strange things to her? He was an ordinary-looking man—nothing unusual about Him. What, then, did He mean by all this?

"Sir," the woman said, "you have nothing to draw with and the well is deep. Where can you get this living water? Are you greater than our father Jacob, who gave us the well and drank from it himself, as did also his sons and his cattle?" Do you know how old this well is? Sixteen hundred years! This is an old water supply! Do you have something better than this sixteen-hundred-year-old well, which has drawn on water that God has supplied? Do you think you can provide me with water, when you don't even have a bucket to lower into this opening? This well is a hundred feet deep and the mouth is seven and a half feet in diameter. How are you going to get down to the water level?

She couldn't understand Jesus. This living water and His talk about the gift of

God left her confused and surprised. But by now she had become curious, and because her curiosity was aroused, she wanted to know more. Jesus drew her into conversation and the barriers that originally stood between them had suddenly disappeared.

Jesus answered, "Everyone who drinks this water will be thirsty again, but whoever drinks the water that I give will never thirst. Indeed, the water I give will become in you a spring of water welling up to eternal life."

Some other water? What other water is there? Not salt water, certainly. That would never do. The well she could see. This well she had known for many years. For sixteen hundred years it had supplied first Jacob's family, then the nomads, the wandering tribes, and now the city of Sychar. What other water is there? What kind of water can quench thirst so completely, that a person need never thirst again? Water welling up to eternal life? A gift of God? And He was going to supply her with this living water? What strange words are these? What is this Jew getting at? She did not know what Jesus was talking about, but she couldn't quiet her curiosity.

The woman said to him, "Sir, give me this water so that I won't get thirsty and have to keep coming here to draw water."

Yes, she'd like that, whatever it is. She didn't appreciate having to carry home these containers of water on her shoulders. When they were full they were heavy, especially in the heat of the day. If she could avoid all this work, her life would be so much easier.

But now that she had committed herself, Jesus changed the subject. He said to her, "Go, call your husband and come back."

"Oh, I see. You want me to call my husband. He's at work. Yes, he is." She stopped for a moment. "Well, actually he is at work, but he is not my husband. I have no husband."

Jesus said to her, "You are right when you say you have no husband. The fact is, you have had five husbands, and the man you now have is not your husband. What you have just said is quite true."

How did He know that? He couldn't have known that about her! She was shocked. Who was He? Some kind of a prophet or something? What was going on here?

Five weddings and no funerals. Yes, she had been married five times in her young life, and none of her husbands had died. She couldn't live with them, or was it the other way around? They couldn't live with her either. Every one of her marriages had turned into a disaster. Five times she had married the wrong man. Or maybe they married the wrong woman? She couldn't keep her husbands, but then she didn't really want to keep them either.

She couldn't stay long in any relationship. She soon tired of it. One year or two. One of her marriages had lasted almost four years. But romance usually flew out the window after the honeymoon. And sometimes during the honeymoon. Being married wasn't so great, after all. Sooner or later all feelings disappeared. They were all alike, those men. They bored her. All they wanted to do after work (one of her husbands didn't even work—he just loafed) was to sit around, drink beer, and watch television. They didn't talk to her. There was no closeness. They weren't interested in anything, except sex. Sex without conversation and sex without love was certainly a turnoff.

So she divorced them—couldn't stand them, didn't want to live with them anymore. It didn't matter what people thought. She didn't care that the women in town avoided her. She dismissed public opinion. And now she was living with this new guy. She had known him for only about six months, and three months ago they moved in together. She didn't want to marry him. Why should she marry again? After five disasters why add another? Isn't five times enough already?

It was time to change the direction of this conversation. Men and marriage were tender subjects for her. This stranger, whoever He was, had no business touching on something so personal. She wanted to avoid this topic. But if He was a prophet (because He knew this stuff about her), then maybe she could ask Him a religious question. He would know something about that.

"Sir," the woman said, "I can see that you are a prophet. Now I have this question that has been bothering me for some time. Our fathers worshiped on this mountain, but you Jews claim that the place where we must worship is in Jerusalem." Why are we Samaritans excluded from worship? And since we are excluded, what is wrong with honoring God on the mountain near the well of father Jacob and in the land of father Abraham? This very land was the land of the patriarchs!

Furthermore, God is the God of the whole world. The Creator of all, the God of all people! Surely this great God will accept all people wherever they live and wherever they choose to call on His name. Are there not many roads to God? Why do the Jews insist that theirs is the world's only true religion?

Jesus declared, "Believe me, woman, a time is coming when you will worship the Father neither on this mountain nor in

Jerusalem." She liked that answer. It didn't sound so biased. But Jesus went on. "You Samaritans worship what you do not know; we worship what we do know, for salvation is from the Jews."

She didn't like that at all. He talked like all the other Israelites who insist on making Jerusalem the exclusive place. These Jews really are prejudiced to think that Samaritans don't know who or what they are worshiping. We Samaritans worship the God of Abraham, Isaac, and Jacob, too.

But she did understand why He would insist that salvation is from the Jews. She knew that the Jews would bring the Messiah to the world—the Messiah who will offer salvation from God. But perhaps the Messiah will bring salvation to the Samaritans as well. She couldn't be sure of that, but her people certainly believe in the coming of the Messiah. She was partly Jewish, of course. Her mother was a half-Jew and her grandmother was an Israelite. Her grandmother had often taught her about the Messiah. That's why she knew about "salvation is from the Jews."

But Jesus was not quite finished answering her question. He said, "A time is coming and has now come when the true worshipers will worship the Father in spirit and truth, for they are the kind of worshipers the Father seeks. God is Spirit, and his worshipers must worship in spirit and truth."

That was better. She agreed with that. Worship should be a spiritual experience, soul to Soul, spirit with Spirit, so to speak.

Well, even if He is some kind of a prophet what does He really know? She was looking for someone more important. Someday the Messiah will straighten out all this confusion. Just like Grandma had said.

The woman said, "I know that Messiah is coming. When He comes, He will explain everything to us."

Who did this strange-talking Jew at Jacob's well think He was? She wanted to put Him in His place. What did He know anyway? She didn't want to accept His words. She believed the Messiah would have all the answers. And she was ready to go back home.

Then Jesus declared, "I who speak to you am He."

That stopped her! She looked up at Him for the first time. She *really* looked at Him. The Messiah? Can it be true? Is He for real? Is this why He talks about living water? Is this why He talks about the gift of God? Is this why He knows about her five weddings and no funerals? Is this why He insists on spiritual worship of God? *He is the Messiah? He is . . . ?*

She turned around abruptly and left her water jar, forgetting the reason why she had come to the well in the first place. The woman went back to the town. She was so excited. It didn't matter that it was a hot day. Her heart was pounding and she was overjoyed!

She said to the people, "Come, see a man who told me everything I ever did. Could this be the Christ?" They came out of the city and made their way toward Him. She didn't get a chance to talk to the women. The fact is she didn't want to speak to the women. She sought out the men and they listened to her—even two of her former husbands who were still in town. She went to the lumberyard where her current lover was working and told him, too. And they came out from Sychar in the middle of the day, right then and there. They could not wait till sundown to see this stranger, this reported Messiah by the well.

"The Messiah," she told them. "He is the Messiah!" No question about it. She was so sure and she repeated some of the conversation, especially that part about her personal life. "He told me all about myself. He offered me living water. I know that sounds strange, but now I know what He means. I feel it in my heart."

Many of the Samaritans from that town believed in him because of the woman's testimony, "He told me everything I ever did." So when the Samaritans came to

> him, they urged him to stay with them, and
> he stayed two days. And because of his
> words many more became believers. They
> said to the woman, "We no longer believe
> just because of what you said; now we have
> heard for ourselves, and we know that this
> man really is the Savior of the world."

Yes, the Savior of the world is here. Not somewhere
else, but here. Jesus comes right into our Samaria,
too—not some other year, but this year; not tomorrow,
but today. Not after all our problems have been re-
solved, but right now He invades our miserable existence. Not after we have cleaned up all our messes, but
while we are still living with someone out of wedlock. He
is the long-awaited Messiah, the Savior who offers living
water. He can touch us and change us, even though He
knows all about us.

Jesus reveals Himself to someone who was not really
looking for Him in the first place! This woman hardly
expected to meet the Messiah on her routine trip to the
well. She was no more looking for God than Gideon was
when an angel visited him. He argued with the Lord before becoming convinced that the Lord would use him to
free the Israelites. Nor did that righteous Pharisee,
Saul of Tarsus, expect a bright light from heaven on the
road to Damascus. He was surprised to hear a voice
asking him, "Why do you persecute me?" He was not
looking for Jesus. The living God approached Gideon
threshing wheat in a winepress, confronted Saul on the
road, and changed a Samaritan woman at Jacob's well.

"He told me all," the woman confessed. God knows
all about me. I cannot hide anything from God. I want

to hide but I can't, because the Lord can see everything in my life. It is true now and it will be true in the future. What we think we have managed to conceal in this life will be laid bare at the judgment. The books will be opened and we will have to give an accounting "on the day when God will judge [people's] secrets through Jesus Christ" (Romans 2:16).

We continue to feel insecure as long as we hold on to our secrets. Being afraid to reveal our sins, we remain without mercy. We are among the unforgiven. But the moment we disclose ourselves we will find acceptance, even as this woman did. When we confess our sins we will be saved. We discover who we really are not by hiding our secrets but by trusting in the grace of Jesus. His mercy creates new people, forgiven and free.

The problem is that we believe we will be loved only when we keep some of our bad stuff hidden. That's how it was when we were children. Didn't we all discover that when we had done something bad it would be better not to tell? When our parents did not know what we had done wrong, they wouldn't correct us or punish us. On the other hand, when we confessed some wrong we were disciplined. Love seemed to be withheld for awhile. Their love was conditional. When we were good, we were accepted. When we were bad, we weren't.

That's why we try so hard to keep the bad stuff hidden from God. We have learned that there are conditions for being accepted and loved. You may have to lie a little. You may have to simply keep quiet. And then we project this conditional love we have experienced in the world to an unconditional God. And that is a big mistake, because God's love is total, complete, and wonderfully unconditional. It is agape, undeserved and freely given because of the very nature of God. As Jesus saw deeply into the soul of the woman at the well and accepted her, so He loves and accepts us too.

When Jesus spoke to Mary Magdalene on that first Easter morning, He called her by name. At that moment Mary realized that Jesus was aware of everything about her. He knew her deeply and personally. With such complete knowledge Jesus did not turn away but approached her, accepted her, and showed that acceptance by calling her name, "Mary." Grasping that truth she responded, "Master." She committed herself as she was seen and known, allowing Him to be the Master of her life.

"He told me all," but did not condemn me. Jesus did not condemn the woman at the well even though she had failed more than once. In spite of her many obvious and painful mistakes she was completely forgiven and fully accepted.

"I felt ashamed of my miserable life," the Samaritan woman probably told her friends, "but Jesus was not ashamed of me. He was even willing to reveal Himself to me as the Messiah. I now feel forgiven and loved and accepted."

Jesus has come to save the world, not to condemn the world—no matter what we have done. All manner of sin can and will be forgiven. Jesus does not count our sins: "One, two, three, four, five, and that's enough. Down you go. You're out!" Not at all. Nothing will be held against us, nothing except the unforgivable sin. Only that sin is unforgivable which is a persistent, willful rejection of the witness of the Spirit—a witness to the salvation Jesus has obtained through His death on the cross and His resurrection from the dead. Not to believe in the Atonement is to pay the price. Every other sin can be wiped away, and your soul will be saved (see Matthew 12:31

The potential of grace is universal.

"He told me all" to bring me to salvation! And so He did. His words touched her soul. They pierced the hardened crust built up by her many failures. That was why Jesus revealed what He knew about her. He did not want to make her feel worse. He sought to bring her to an acceptance of reality, to a new life. The purpose of opening this painful subject was for her own good. And He reached that goal. He is the Savior of the world, after all. That is why Jesus has come—to save us and bring us to eternal life.

It is all of grace. It is absolutely free!

So don't insult God by trying to pay for your salvation by doing good works. Good works can never make up for your sins. You cannot even the score by works. All you can do, like the woman at the well, is to accept the forgiveness and mercy of the Messiah. Good works are the result of faith. They do not create faith nor do they achieve acceptance with God. We are to do good works after we receive the free grace of God. It is by grace alone, as the Samaritan woman discovered, that we are saved and made whole. "It is by grace you have been saved through faith—and this not from yourselves. It is the gift of God" (Ephesians 2:8).

Little did she know that on her routine trip to the well on that hot but ordinary day she would move from annoyance at seeing Him to curiosity because He talked about living water. From curiosity she would progress to embarrassment about her past. And from embarrassment she would become defiant since she didn't like His answers to her religious question. And finally she advanced from defiance to faith.

"Come, see a man who told me everything! He must be the Messiah. He has touched and changed my life!"

> Don't be under any illusion—neither the impure, the idolater or the adulterer; neither the effeminate, the pervert or the thief; neither the swindler, the drunkard, the foul-mouthed or the rapacious shall have any share in the kingdom of God. *And such . . . were some of you!* But you have cleansed yourselves from all that, you have been made whole in spirit, you have been justified in the name of the Lord Jesus and in the Spirit of our God.
>
> *1 Corinthians 6:9* PHILLIPS

[Jesus] came to a town in Samaria called Sychar, near the plot of ground Jacob had given to his son Joseph. Jacob's well was there, and Jesus, tired as he was from the journey, sat down by the well. It was about the sixth hour.

Then a Samaritan woman came to draw water, Jesus said to her, "Will you give me a drink?" (His disciples had gone into the town to buy food.)

The Samaritan woman said to him, "You are a Jew and I am a Samaritan woman. How can you ask me for a drink?" (For Jews do not associate with Samaritans.)

Jesus answered her, "If you knew the gift of God and who it is that asks you for a drink, you would have asked him and he would have given you living water."

"Sir," the woman said, "you have nothing to draw with and the well is deep. Where can you get this living water? Are you greater than our father Jacob, who gave us the well and drank from it himself, as did also his sons and his flocks and herds?"

Jesus answered, "Everyone who drinks this water will be thirsty again, but whoever drinks the water I give him will never thirst. Indeed, the water I give him will become in him a spring of water welling up to eternal life."

The woman said to him, "Sir, give me this water so that I won't get thirsty and have to keep coming here to draw water."

He told her, "Go, call your husband and come back."

"I have no husband," she replied.

Jesus said to her, "You are right when you say you have no husband. The fact is, you have had five husbands, and the man you now have is not your husband. What you have just said is quite true."

"Sir," the woman said, "I can see that you are a prophet. Our fathers worshiped on this mountain, but you Jews claim that the place where we must worship is in Jerusalem."

Jesus declared, "Believe me, woman, a time is coming when you will worship the Father neither on this mountain nor in Jerusalem. You Samaritans worship what you do not know; we worship what we do know, for salvation is from the Jews. Yet a time is coming and has now come when the true worshipers will worship the Father in spirit and truth, for they are the kind of worshipers the Father seeks.

God is spirit, and his worshipers must worship in spirit and in truth."

The woman said, "I know that Messiah (called Christ) is coming. When he comes, he will explain everything to us."

Then Jesus declared, "I who speak to you am he."

Leaving her water jar, the woman went back to the town and said to the people, "Come, see a man who told me everything I ever did. Could this be the Christ?" They came out of the town and made their way toward him.

Many of the Samaritans from that town believed in him because of the woman's testimony, "He told me everything I ever did." So when the Samaritans came to him, they urged him to stay with them, and he stayed two days. And because of his words many more became believers.

They said to the woman, "We no longer believe just because of what you said; now we have heard for ourselves, and we know that this man really is the Savior of the world."

John 4:5

A Lost Soul

There is in Jerusalem near the Sheep Gate a pool that in Aramaic is called Bethesda and that is surrounded by five covered colonnades. Here a great number of disabled people used to lie—the blind, the lame, the paralyzed.

What a sight of suffering humanity!—as if the hospitals had been emptied out and all the hurting sick and afflicted lay there outdoors in the space by the pool and in the open street. Broken people too weak to help themselves, the chronically ill, the terminally ill, victims of diverse diseases—without medical care, their condition worsened every day; they lay moaning and crying out in agony and pain.

But they congregated in that place because they had a glimmer of hope. Just the slightest glimmer was sufficient to keep them there in expectation waiting for the moving of the waters. From time to time an angel of the Lord would come down and stir up the waters. The one into the pool after each such disturbance would be cured of whatever disease he or she had.

Just a faint ray of hope, like the first hint of dawn before the rising sun, yet the promise was not for everyone; it was for only one poor, suffering soul there. When the water trembled, that was the signal for a miraculous healing for one person—no matter what the infirmity. The illness was not the issue. Any kind of disorder could be healed. But it was for only the *first* person to enter the pool. Why only one? Why did God allow so many to suffer and heal so few? Why does God permit so much misery? Why can't everyone be made whole? Even though there was hope for one, the pool held no answers for those questions, no answers at all.

One who was there had been an invalid for thirty-eight years—thirty-eight years out there on the same street! All those years waiting for a new troubling of the waters! Unbelievable. Thirty-eight years, and he was *still* there—still held a flicker of hope? He started his first trek to the pool when he was seventeen. Now he was fifty-five years old and certainly no better. His physical condition had not improved, and mentally he was deteriorating—more bitter, more cynical, more fearful, more despairing, more disturbed, more despondent—more questions.

Why did he continue to come? Was there any chance for him to be healed after all this time, after all these years? The fact is there was nowhere else for him to go. This pool was the only place for people like him. He had nothing else to look forward to in life, not in his miserable existence—nothing.

When Jesus saw him lying there and learned he had been in this condition for a long time, He asked him, "Do you want to get well?"

Wait a minute, sir. Are you serious? Of course I want to get well. Do you really think I enjoy being sick? Who wouldn't want to be delivered from pain and discomfort? Of course I want relief from my lame leg and my bad back. I can't walk straight anymore. And I limp badly. I don't want to stay like this. But it's not as easy as all that, is it? Just because I want to be healed doesn't it make it so, now does it? I have been looking for a healing for a long time. Do you know how long? But nothing has ever happened. Nothing has ever changed.

You see, sir, I may want to be healed. But what good is it to have this desire? Isn't healing up to God? I can't make God give me good health. No one else can help me. Sir, I've prayed about this, but God has not heard my prayers. God is not moved. God doesn't even take notice of me. Do I want to get well? Of course I do. But unless God pays attention to me, there's no hope for me at all.

Don't try to arouse any false hopes
here—not for this poor man. Not now.

"Sir," the invalid replied, "I have no
one to help me into the pool when the water is stirred. While I am trying to get in,
someone else goes ahead of me."

It's the same, old story, sir. All these
years now I've tried to get into the pool before other people, but I've never made it.
I'll tell you the same thing I've told everyone else. I become weary of repeating this
same story. Are you sure you want to hear
my reasons? I've never been able to get
into the pool quickly enough. Others push
ahead of me. It's my back, sir, as I told
you, and one of my legs is lame. That's
why I hobble when I walk. By the time I
make it into the pool, it's too late. That's
the trouble.

We repeatedly tell our tales of woe to whoever will
listen, because the tales get attention. Sometimes we receive sympathy. People get choked up by them, because the more we rehearse, the better we get at the
telling: "Let me tell you about what happened to me
when . . . " Our families have heard these sob stories a
hundred times. Our children feel like screaming, "Not
that same old story again!" But we repeat the yarn because it is familiar and safe.

I can't step into the water, sir. You see,
as I've told you, it's my legs and my back.
So what are my chances for a miracle? Not

very good, right? God knows, I've tried. But I'm too slow. That's the trouble. Someone else scrambles into the water before me. That's just my luck. I guess I'm not supposed to be healed. I'm never going to feel normal again. That's my lot, I suspect.

We all have our stories.

"I'm plagued with headaches. They have been with me all my life. The older I get, the worse my headaches become. It'll never change. I don't have much hope."

"I'm slow. I just don't move fast. I know it takes me longer than most people to get things done. I often run late for my appointments or for church. I just can't seem to change that. I get sidetracked. Start one job and then skip to another. That's just the way I am. I've learned to accept it."

"I'm HIV positive. I know I made some mistakes in my life. I certainly didn't mean to get this, but I know that now it's downhill for me. Slowly, but still downhill. I don't have any great expectations. Not much hope. I'll do my best to live with it."

"I was abused as a child. It was real bad. I've suffered all my life because of that. I've been in counseling, but I am the product of a dysfunctional family, and I can't get rid of my past. God knows I've tried."

We have learned to play victim. We carry the results of what people have done to us, how they have treated us. Whether it was parents, family, neighbors, friends, teachers, or society, the result is the same. We are victims because of them or because of a serious illness, an accident, a death even, something we could do nothing about—outside forces.

Or perhaps you did it to yourself. You took the drugs. You swallowed the drinks. You ran with the wrong crowd. You were tempted and were not strong enough to resist the temptation. You are responsible and you know it. Now you are hopelessly caught, a victim of your foolish, self-centered, and indulgent life.

Who will deliver you from this predicament? No one will carry you into the pool at the opportune time. Someone else always gets there ahead of you. You're too late, and that's why you feel so alone in your pain. No one talks to you. No one takes notice of you there in the street. No one seems to care for you. The traffic just passes you by. Only Jesus comes over to see how you are.

Can we ask some questions here? Where was this poor soul's wife? Why was she not with him? Couldn't she have helped him? Did he even ask for her help, or was he too discouraged to involve her? Was their marriage in trouble? Had it been in trouble for years? And what about his children? Why didn't they give him a hand? He had a strong and healthy son—played line on the high school football team. He was muscular and could have lifted his dad into the pool handily. Was there no one in his family he could call on? He had brothers and uncles and cousins, too—all kinds of relatives. Where were they when the waters in the pool started to move?

What about his friends, for that matter? Why was he lying there all alone among the other sick people in the portico? Was he cantankerous? crotchety? difficult to live with? obnoxious? unattractive? Did he have a weight problem? Did he have a disgusting habit? Did he smell? Was he like some people who can't get friends or family to lend them a hand because nobody likes them? At least the disabled man in another story had friends who brought him to Jesus, broke up a roof, and lowered Joe into the living room. But this poor soul couldn't rouse anyone. Maybe he was just an odious, offensive person.

So why did Jesus have to go so far afield to reach out for someone like that person? Why did Jesus seek out this obscure, abandoned, hopeless victim, this forgotten and lonely, friendless man? Why does Jesus reach out to people like that—the seemingly useless, unimportant nobodies who exist on the fringes of society? Does Jesus not have any limits? Does Jesus really respect every person? Does He actually want to give every last one of us an opportunity at life and salvation? Does this mean we all have a chance—even if no one else pays any attention to us?

> Jesus said to him, "Get up! Pick up your mat and walk."

Notice something. Jesus does not lift him into the pool. Jesus does not give the man what the man thinks he needs for healing, that is, to get into the water. Jesus is unconventional. He simply tells the man to get up. That's what He wants him to do. God doesn't do things my way, the way I expect God to do them. God heals in His own way, because His ways are not mine: "'My thoughts are not your thoughts, neither are your ways my ways,' declares the Lord" (Isaiah 55:8). And as it turns out, God's way is far better than mine!

Jesus doesn't even say to this individual, "Listen to Me. Look at Me. Believe in Me. You can forget about the

pool, because you don't need the pool," nor does He tell
this negative sinner who has all kinds of reasons why
nothing has worked for him in thirty-eight years, "repent and believe; come now and confess your sins." No.
Jesus only instructs the man to get up.

Jesus started off by reaching deep down into the
soul with His probing question: "Do you want to get
well?" This frustrated, discouraged man objected, argued, resisted, complained, and explained, but Jesus
had touched his heart and stirred a hidden, secret longing. We may sound negative. We may spin excuses. We
may speak with skepticism, but all that hardness is on
the surface. Beneath that outer shell is a soft center. In
my heart I want to be accepted and forgiven. I want to
be healed.

And now Jesus follows up that simple question by
telling him to get up. It's as simple as that. First, do you
want to be healed? Then, get up! So also, do you want
to be saved? Then "believe in the Lord Jesus, and you
will be saved" (Acts 16:31). Do you want eternal life?
"Everyone who looks to the Son and believes in him
[will] have eternal life" (John 6:40).

> Do you want me to get up?
> Yes.
> Right here?
> Yes.
> Right now?
> Yes.
> Don't you want me to step into the
> pool?
> No.
> You want me to stand up and walk

away, when I haven't been able to move
without help in thirty-eight years?

Yes.

Do you believe I can do it?

Yes.

I don't know if I can.

You can do it. *Do you want to get
well?*

Of course I do, sir. I do.

Give the poor man credit. He did it—after all those
years. He looked right at Jesus, straightened his lame
leg slowly, pushed himself up, and actually stood up. He
was willing to do whatever he was asked to do.

So, there he stood—smiling—picked
up his pallet, and walked away.

But the day on which this took place
was a Sabbath, and so the Jews said to the
man who had been healed, "It is the Sabbath; the law forbids you to carry your
mat."

Not lawful? Not *lawful?* Do these god-
ly leaders realize what has happened to
this poor soul who had been lying there for
thirty-eight years? This was a new beginning for him! He had been healed on this
very special day, Sabbath or not. What
difference did it make that this was the
Sabbath? Could any law forbid him to feel
so good and so thankful? Could they not
bend the rules a little? This was a glorious
victory for him! A lost soul had been

found. Why should he not carry his bed-roll and let everyone know the power of God?

He replied, "The man who made me well said to me, 'Pick up your mat and walk.' "

He had been wondrously healed. And should he not listen to the person who had healed him? The healer told him to pick up his bedroll. Why should he not obey Him? What was wrong with that? Do you want me to leave it there in the street? That wouldn't be right either, would it? Besides, it belongs to me, and I'll need it again to sleep in tonight. Of course I'm going to do what He tells me. I'm walking normal again! After thirty-eight years, sir, I'm walking. This is the greatest day of my life!

They asked him, "Who is this fellow who told you to pick it up and walk?" The man who was healed had no idea who it was, for Jesus had slipped away into the crowd that was there.

The man did not even know who Jesus was! He had never heard of Him. He was unaware there was a Savior in Jerusalem! Evidently he knew nothing of Jesus' signs and wonders. He had not been privy to conversations about this prophet from Ga-lilee or His miracles, nor that some thought Him to be the Son of David. No one had mentioned to him that the Messiah could be visiting Jerusalem. He did not know the first thing about Jesus, because he had sunk into his miserable life all by himself in complete isolation by that pool with the five porches.

And yet he responded to Jesus. He heard the question, he wanted to be made whole, but he did not know anything about the stranger who talked with him. And this means that *anyone* could have asked him, "Do you want to be healed?"

James Forbes, the gifted preacher of Riverside Church, New York, relates an early experience when he preached the sermon at a Kathryn Kuhlman healing crusade. Miss Kuhlman told the pastors there, "You can be healers too if you let the power of God work through you," which the pastors found hard to believe. In fact, at her large crusades it was she who invited people to come forward. She was the only instrument of God for miracles of healing. No one else.

After that particular service a couple approached James Forbes. The woman confided that they had attended the crusade for her husband's hearing problem. Now Forbes had preached about a man in the Gospels who was hard of hearing. Jesus had said to that man, "Ephphatha!" which means, "Be opened." The woman told Forbes that her husband had been waiting anxiously for the sermon to be over with so he could go forward and receive healing from Kathryn Kuhlman. But he had actually started to hear during the sermon at the word "Ephphatha!"

"That was an extraordinary lesson for me," confessed Dr. Forbes. He realized that anyone can be an instrument of God (James Forbes, *The Holy Spirit and Preaching* [Nashville: Abingdon Press, 1989], p. 98). Healers are not the only ones God uses! Anyone can ask, "Do you want to be made whole?" That is the startling truth of this healing story in the Gospels. Without credentials, Jesus brought this lost soul to salvation.

But our story is not quite finished.

> After the fact, the lost soul was worshiping in the temple when Jesus made a point of looking for him. Jesus found him and said to him, "See, you are well again. Stop sinning or something worse may happen to you."

They met in the temple, which is a good place to go after your healing. In the temple you give thanks to God that, after all these years of distress, He has released you from your anguish. God has actually brought renewal to your body and your soul.

But why did Jesus tell him, "Stop sinning or something worse may happen to you"? What can be worse than thirty-eight years of agony? Isn't that enough? What does Jesus have in mind? If we are to take His words at face value, the only thing worse is not more pain and sorrow here, but separation from God throughout eternity. No life, no love, no peace forever is the only thing worse than suffering here.

What does Jesus mean by this injunction to "stop sinning"? What connection is there between the man's sin and his suffering, if any? Are we punished in our bodies because of our sins? Is sickness always a penalty for evil deeds? Can that really be true?

Surely that is not the teaching of Jesus. His disciples once asked Him why a blind man had been born that way. Was it because of his sins or his parents' sins? Who, if anyone, was to blame? Jesus' answer is clear. Neither had the blind man nor his parents been responsible for his blindness. They were sinners to be sure, but that did not mean they or anyone else was accountable for his blindness (see John 9:2 a reason was to be found it had to do with the purpose and glory of God. Surely, then, Jesus does not intimate, not in the slightest, that this man has been tormented for thirty-eight years because of his sins.

What, then, is the meaning of "stop sinning"? Consider this man's decades-long defeated and hopeless state of mind. He was downright discouraged. Maybe he had a good reason to be depressed. And who among us would blame him for feeling this way? But he lacked faith. He felt hopeless. He neglected prayer. Why did he complain so much? Why was he unable to get someone to lift him into the pool? Had he lost all his initiative? Would he be able to change now? Could he become a more positive person? more hopeful? Could he develop a better attitude? Could he begin to believe in God, now that his body was functioning in a normal way? That was the point!

Stop sinning—in thought and attitude and word and deed. Trust in the living God. Believe in the Savior. The one who has healed you loves you. Salvation is a new way of life, a new life in Christ. What you have heard about peace and joy is good news. What you have heard about power and courage are the promises of God. You are not being asked to have your old self patched up. A new, creative act of the Spirit pronounces you a child of

God. That is the meaning of "stop sinning." You are not required to live a sinless life, but you can make a commitment to the living Christ. He is Lord. He will give you a new attitude, a new direction, a new dynamic.

This "stop sinning" is not a heavy burden laid on us. We already have the Ten Commandments, which is more than enough. "Stop sinning" is a new power provided by "Christ in you, the hope of glory" (Colossians 1:27). It does not mean trying to do better with the old life in the flesh, but it means receiving the new life in the Spirit. "Stop sinning" is a command of hope, since the Spirit of God has been given us.

When you become a Christian, according to the apostle Peter, you have "purified yourselves by obeying the truth" (1 Peter 1:22). This means that because of God's gift of grace, you are forgiven, approved, and already purified. Your sins are washed away. You are accepted. In that purity you will enter glory. Nothing less will do! So purity becomes a new way of life.

That is why the question "Do you want to get well?" leads to the statement, "Stop sinning." Jesus wants to change your life, not just improve it. This is the meaning of salvation. This is the call of God to eternal life.

Our story comes to a brief conclusion.

> The man went away and told the Jews
> that it was Jesus who had made him well.
> So, because Jesus was doing these things
> on the Sabbath, the Jews persecuted him.

Can you believe that? What is this? How can it be? Jesus has healed this man, delivered him from a disas-

trous thirty-eight years, and they are more interested in
technicalities than actualities! They are more concerned about one law than the salvation of a person? In
their pious opinion Jesus has broken a law. He has des-
ecrated the Sabbath—never mind that a miserable life
has been wonderfully changed. Never mind that a lost
soul has been found. Never mind that someone has been
rescued from the pit.

Because the Jews were obsessed by this breaking of
a law, Jesus cannot qualify as a holy man. The good He
accomplishes is totally rejected by them. He will be persecuted for breaking sacred laws that God had estab-
lished. Holy people are to obey the holy law to the letter,
so why does Jesus not behave like every good Jew is supposed to behave? Who does He think He is to set Himself above the law of God?

What kind of thinking is this? Do we fall into a similar trap when we elevate technicalities of law above actualities—say, in our legal system, when a person who
is guilty of a terrible crime is released because of a legal
technicality? And do we also make similar mistakes in
religion when we fail to consider Jesus Christ as our
Savior and Lord, because we have been offended by
some church member? or we may have witnessed hypoc-
risy in a Christian, so we refuse to come to Christ because of it?

Even so, this incident at the pool in Jerusalem shows
us one person who is saved. Jesus touches his life and
makes him whole. "The Son of Man came to seek and to
save what was lost" (Luke 19:11). This good news is for
Zacchaeus with all his money, as well as for this lost soul
who had none. Jesus is not impressed by reputation,
achievement, nor station in life. He is not shocked by

your past, your failures, nor your despair. He looks into your soul and knows your deepest anguish. He offers holy help and healing. The Son of God has power to make you well.

Jesus comes to you now and asks, "Do you want to get well?" And if you allow that question to touch your heart, you will be saved. He reaches you where you are hurting, where you feel hopeless and really desperate. He knows how to penetrate to the one place where you always hoped someone would touch you—at the core of your being—in your soul. And suddenly you realize Jesus has opened up something you have kept under lock and key for years. There, deep inside you is the desire, the need, the longing for God. And now you realize also that if anyone can touch you there, it must be God!

Do you want to be made whole? It is a simple question, and it begs a simple answer. "Yes, I do" is all it takes. That's all it took for that lost man in Jerusalem so many years ago. Jesus seeks you out from among all the other sufferers in the world. Yes, He loves them too, but He is looking for you, there in the crowded street.

And you thought no one would ever pay attention to you. You thought no one cares. You thought you were hopeless.

Do you want to get well? Then get up. Stop sinning

Now there is in Jerusalem near the Sheep Gate a pool, which in Aramaic is called Bethesda and which is surrounded by five covered colonnades. Here a great number of disabled people used to lie—the blind, the lame, the paralyzed. One who was there had been an invalid for thirty-eight years. When Jesus saw him lying there and learned that he had been in this condition for a long time, he asked him, "Do you want to get well?"

"Sir," the invalid replied, "I have no one to help me into the pool when the water is stirred. While I am trying to get in, someone else goes down ahead of me."

Then Jesus said to him, "Get up! Pick up your mat and walk." At once the man was cured; he picked up his mat and walked.

The day on which this took place was a Sabbath, and so the Jews said to the man who had been healed, "It is the Sabbath; the law forbids you to carry your mat."

But he replied, "The man who made me well said to me, 'Pick up your mat and walk.'"

So they asked him, "Who is this fellow who told you to pick it up and walk?"

The man who was healed had no idea who it was, for Jesus had slipped away into the crowd that was there.

Later Jesus found him at the temple and said to him, "See, you are well again. Stop sinning or something worse may happen to you." The man went away and told the Jews that it was Jesus who had made him well.

So, because Jesus was doing these things on the Sabbath, the Jews persecuted him.

John 5:2

The Alien

Jesus withdrew to the region of Tyre and Sidon. A Canaanite from that vicinity came to Him. Let's call her Marge. Marge had heard about Jesus, but she never dreamed she would have the privilege of seeing Him. He helped people down south in Galilee, while she lived near the Mediterranean Sea, in a small village close to the seaport of Tyre. Nor was she Jewish, but she had heard of the wonderful miracles of this Jesus who had healed so many people of various diseases. He had been the talk of the region for some time now, and then she'd heard the good news—He had actually crossed the border into her country.

What had brought Him to this region? The reason really didn't matter to Marge. The good news was that He was *here*. She had decided to see Him, especially if He was headed toward the coast, and she would bring her daughter with her. She would take her chances of pressing through the crowd with her request.

She cried out to him, "Lord, Son of David, have mercy on me! My daughter is suffering terribly from demon-possession."

Yes, Marge was in trouble. Her daughter was in trouble. For years the girl had been unmanageable and no one—not even a specialist—could find a formula for calming her down. She was hyperactive. At times she would scream as loud as she could, for no apparent reason. Did she need drugs or medication? They tried everything. For awhile some new treatment would lift everyone's hopes, but then the girl would revert to her old habits, with the same defiant rebellion. At last, one of the doctors told Marge, "Frankly, we think she has a demon, and we have no remedy for demon-possession."

Whatever it was, her daughter was a handful, a stubborn, rebellious, strong-willed child. She seemed unable to respond to simple requests. When Marge directed her, the girl would try to listen and obey. But she'd soon forget her good intentions. She seemed unable to carry them out. She would repeat the patterns again and again, and she seemed to defy all authority. She behaved as though she had never heard her mother's rules and regulations, few as they were.

The daughter was also diagnosed as having a learning disability. At school she had to be placed in a special class. The girl tried to make friends but she was seldom able to keep them. She was too self-centered, her own worst enemy. She wanted her own way and alienated other children with her temper tantrums. At home the youngster sometimes retreated to her room and when Mother walked in, she would find the girl sobbing uncontrollably.

"What's wrong?"

"Nothing."

"Why are you crying?"

"I don't know."

"Can't you talk about it to Mommy?"

"No." And more convulsive sobs.

The girl didn't improve when she reached her teens. Things only became worse. Soon she was running around with the wrong crowd, so eager to make friends she headed down dangerous roads. She experimented with drugs. She drank. At an early age she became sexually active, in a desperate attempt to gain love and acceptance. Everything went wrong in her life and she realized she was a disappointment to her family. She knew that she was a burden to her mother, but she did not know how to change—nor did she want to. Maybe it was some kind of possession after all.

But where was Marge's husband? Marge had become pregnant and he had insisted on marriage. Even though he assured her of his love, she always believed he felt obligated to give their baby a name. There was another factor. Her husband was Jewish and she was a Canaanite. That became another strike against them. Neither family accepted them at first. They were all opposed to the marriage, and the coming of a baby produced great tension. So the couple ran away for a quick ceremony performed by a justice of the peace, which didn't please either family.

So it wasn't under the best of circumstances that they became a family, and it certainly didn't help that in their village everyone knew everyone else—and everyone else's business. The marriage lasted for almost eight years. That was long enough for him. He said he couldn't take it anymore, not with the problem child they were raising.

So the Canaanite had no husband to help her now. He had walked out on both of them, moved away, and was not heard from again. His hurt and suffering were too deep. Marge thought how often trials penetrate to the core of our beings. Our pain is hidden in small corners. We both feel so terribly hurt. We cannot cope. And so he had resorted to escape. The damage is done and it affects us all.

The daughter knows she is a burden to others, her mother cannot cope with the rebellion, and her father skips out because he cannot handle the problem. Even the extended family—grandparents, brothers, sisters, cousins—suffer disgrace and offer little help.

One thing her husband had contributed to the marriage was his heritage. He acquainted his wife with the Jews and their religion. She didn't know anything about these people, except what she had learned in school. In her history classes she had read about the golden age of these Jews and their kings named David and Solomon. And now, her husband had told her, they were looking for a Messiah, a deliverer who would save not only the Jews, but also the whole world. This Savior would bring peace to all people and come from the lineage of that very good king named David. He was to be known as "the Son of David."

That much Marge had learned. That much she believed. So, when she heard that Jesus of Nazareth was being called "the Son of David," she knew what it meant. When He entered her country, her mind was made up. She would not let this once-in-a-lifetime opportunity slip through her fingers.

So it was that this woman, bringing her troubled daughter with her, came to Jesus. The teenager didn't resist. She was willing to come since she was in one of her more mellow moods. For that, Marge was thankful.

She knew how to address Him: "Lord, Son of David, have mercy on me!"

Jesus did not answer a word. He ignored her, paid no attention to her, acted as if she wasn't there, as if He had not heard her plea. Why? Had the Messiah not appeared for all people, as her husband assured her? Had the Messiah not come from God, the God who created the whole world? Was not this Creator God loving and caring? Why, then, would the Messiah be deaf to her plea, refusing to show mercy and compassion? Surely God is not prejudiced or one-dimensional!

Or did He act like this because she was a woman and He was a man? Do Jewish men always look down on foreign women? But surely women have rights too! The good news is not only for males, is it? Of course not. She had heard that Jesus cared about women down there in Galilee, that He healed and helped women and was wonderful with children.

But this was not about her. This was about her daughter, who had recently turned sixteen. Both of them, mother and daughter, had suffered for so many years because the girl was afflicted and tormented. Or was it because of demon-possession? No one knew what to do about her problems. Marge was at a loss, but she would not be put off at this point—not as easily as that. She would not simply fade away. Even though Jesus ignored her, she kept on calling out to Him from the crowd.

His disciples urged Him, "Send her away, for she keeps crying out after us."

She didn't like the disciples at all. They acted as if they were His bodyguards, as if they had to protect Him from people. They were like a wall between her and the Son of David. They didn't want her anywhere near Him. They were not very understanding. They certainly lacked compassion. They would not allow her to approach Jesus, to talk to Him, and she didn't appreciate the fact that they kept her at a distance. They were interfering needlessly. She was no threat to anyone.

But how could they understand what she had endured all these years? How could they know the trouble her little girl had caused for everyone in her young life? They had not lived through sixteen miserable years. So how could they understand her compulsion to see Jesus now? How could they, unless they had raised a disobedient, rebellious, and willful child?

Anyway, she didn't care about the disciples. She had not come to see them. She just wanted to get through to Jesus. She tried pushing her way in, but these men were stronger than she was. She considered biting one of them on the arm and clawing her way through with her nails, but she restrained herself. All the while she kept on crying out, begging Jesus to pay attention to her. But He seemed not to notice her.

She wouldn't stop. She refused to take no for an answer. Not now. Not after all these troublesome years of agony and suffering. He had to pay attention to her needs.

Jesus answered, "I was sent only to the lost sheep of Israel." Not to anyone else. Not to outsiders, only insiders.

Well, at least He heard her. He acknowledged her. He did respond to her. He was not a brick wall, like those bodyguards around Him. And that confirmed something else: she was not being rejected because she was a woman, nor did Jesus turn her down because of her daughter. The reason was clear now: she was not Jewish. That was the problem! He affirmed that His ministry was for His own people.

But if His only interest was in reaching the Jews, then why had Jesus crossed the border into this foreign country? Not for those few Jews who had settled in her land—they were too sparse. What about her and her people, even though they didn't belong to His so-called sheep? Now that He was here, couldn't He help her, too?

God is the Creator of the whole world! God is a God of love who loves all people on earth, is that not true? Surely this God cannot single out only those Jews down south? If the love of God is only for the Jews, why should all His creation be excluded from salvation? Surely that cannot be true. That cannot be the case. That is unfair to the inhabitants of earth, and God is not unfair. She did not believe that God is a respecter of persons. That cannot be true!

That is why she took fresh courage from Jesus' words.

Marge came and knelt before Him. "Lord, help me!" she said. She was not going to relent. She could not possibly conceive of giving up. She had pushed her way through the strong wall of those disciples, and now Jesus did pay attention to her. Even if she had to grovel at His feet, it would be all right. She really believed that He was her only hope. He alone could do something for her daughter, could free her of this possession. And now she was on her face there in front of Jesus, with her teenage daughter standing directly behind her. They were both looking at Him.

Jesus replied, "It is not right to take the children's bread and toss it to their dogs."

These Jews could be insulting! She knew that Jews thought of themselves as God's chosen people. They looked down on everyone else. They had a certain arrogance about them because they thought they were special. But there was no excuse for it.

Why had Jesus compared her to a dog? Whatever He meant, His choice of words bothered her. These Jews must think they're God's gift to the world. She realized they were like that, and it troubled her that Jesus, the Son of David, sounded like this too.

In spite of her first thoughts she refused to take it as an insult. Maybe He meant that the children had to be fed before the animals could be fed. Maybe all He was doing was using an example of how it is in a family, giving an illustration. That was a better way to look at His words. Then He was not really calling her a dog.

As an illustration this made sense, after all. It had been true in her childhood home. Her parents were poor and they sometimes couldn't afford to buy enough food. Times were tough, so the children were always fed first, then the adults. If anything was left for the animals, that was well and good, but the animals could always scrounge around for food. Her parents usually didn't have money to buy dog food or cat food.

Well, if this Jesus is the Son of David, if He is the promised Messiah, if He comes from God, then He must be here for her, too. Marge firmly believed this. She too belonged to the human race. She too was created in the image of God. God is not *against* people; He is *for* us. So she would see it through. Under no circumstances would she disappear with a sad face into the crowd.

Nor was she about to argue with Jesus. This was hardly the time for disagreements. She would accept whatever He said. She would take her place, humbly.

It's not right to take the children's bread and toss it to their dogs, He'd said.

"Yes, Lord," she answered, "but even the dogs eat the crumbs that fall from their masters' table." I'll fall on my face and I'll say anything you want. I'll do anything to receive those crumbs.

She didn't mind humbling herself. She wanted to gain Jesus' approval. She would accept the scraps that fell from the table. She would do anything to get relief for her daughter's afflicted and tormented soul.

Those pathetic bits and pieces, those few crumbs? She would receive them, gladly, just as the animals eagerly, gratefully, heartily gobbled up whatever came their way. Yes, the food came down from above.

Surely you have tasted some humiliation, too. Surely you have come up against situations beyond your control. You know what shame is about. Do you realize how life changing these events can become? They reveal our weaknesses and make us feel vulnerable. And it is from that position of weakness not of strength that we cry out for help. The salvation that comes from God is given to the weak and needy. God does not come near to the proud, but only to the humble—never to those with a false humility. Faking humility is another form of pride. "The devil did grin, for his darling sin is pride which apes humility."

Writing to the Christians in Rome, the apostle Paul becomes very candid in the middle of his letter. He writes that he could never save himself and that even after his salvation he is unable to live the Christian life. "I do not understand what I do. For what I want to do I do not do, but what I hate I do. . . . I know that nothing good lives in me, that is, in my sinful nature. For I have the desire to do what is good, but I cannot carry it out" (Romans 7:15). That is a sobering thought and it leads us to confession of sin and into true humility.

The meek will inherit the earth. No one else has a chance.

And now after the Canaanite accepted His terms and played His game, how long did she have to wait for Jesus to answer her? Who knows? I think there was a long pause. Only afterward came that wonderful, exhilarating moment!

> Jesus answered, "Woman, you have great faith! Your request is granted." And her daughter was healed from that very hour!
>
> Oh, yes. It was true. Her daughter was healed! She got what she wanted! He heard her request and gave her her heart's desire. What a stimulating conclusion to her persistent and earnest prayer!

Jesus is compassionate, after all. He reaches down to where we are, because we cannot reach up to where

He is. We cannot save ourselves. God enters the world and comes into our midst. Having invaded this humble existence, He calls all who are meek and lowly in heart. He does not shout commandments from heaven above, but lays aside His glory and suffers with us on earth. He reaches down to lift us up.

"Woman, you have great faith." You have shown me that you believe, no matter how many roadblocks I have put in your way. You have demonstrated that you will persevere until you receive what you want. And that kind of active, persistent faith will be rewarded. Because you desire so much, believe so much, the misery of sixteen years is history.

And now in all probability Jesus takes her by the hand, pulls her to her feet and possibly gives her a hug. Then He touches and includes her daughter in the divine love before He turns to someone else who has a problem. The girl is miraculously healed.

Again and again in the gospel stories the power of God is revealed by the Son of God, but this time it takes place in a foreign land, among strangers to the covenant, among aliens to the people of God. This miracle assures us that no one is excluded from the love and mercy of God, for the covenant is about to include the whole world! This is just as the Canaanite had hoped all along. The Messiah has come with an open invitation to salvation, to the Jew first but also for the Gentile.

All this is true even for those who feel left out—foreigners, aliens, strangers to the promises of God. Foreigners are now included in the new covenant and are called citizens of the kingdom of God. Aliens become joint heirs with the chosen people. Strangers from far join friends from nearby to form the one body of

Christ. Outsiders join insiders. All who respond in faith belong to the body, and every part of that body counts.

"Once you were not a people, but now you are the people of God; once you had not received mercy, but now you have received mercy" (1 Peter 2:10). It was gloriously true for that alien in our gospel story, and so it is for those of another race or color who are converted from another religion. The mercy of God is extended to the whole creation. The body of Christ is even named "the bride of Christ." Other citizens will join with the saints and are accorded an equal place in heaven. That is the exaltation for the humble!

Oh, yes. She would not be denied. She persisted against all odds. She had to get through to Jesus. She believed that He was her only hope. Everything else had failed. Jesus once illustrated persistence in prayer with a story about a farmer's friend who came knocking at the farmer's door one night. He bothered this farmer at midnight because he had unexpected out-of-town guests and had no bread to feed them for breakfast. This friend kept on knocking, bothering the sleepy farmer, disturbing the people in the house, until he got results. That was all there was to it. And as we have seen, this alien woman was not going to relent either. She had dogged determination.

Marge had to do it for her daughter. Her daughter could not change herself. Something possessed her, and it had to be cast out. This is how we are to pray. Give us this day our daily bread. Even if I'm not sitting at table with the family, I will take the scraps that fall from the table. Whatever I can get. I'll accept that. You must hear my prayer for my daughter's healing!

As mother and daughter headed home, Marge reflected on the events of the day. It was only then that she realized the full impact of what had taken place. She enjoyed rethinking her steps, playing them over and over in her mind, with the wonderful results of that visit to Jesus. Only now did she realize how life changing this experience had been. After all these years there was healing and salvation. Sixteen years were history. She was sure it was real. She was sure it would last. Her daughter seemed calm, in her right mind, sweet and kind. This miracle was indeed God's doing.

At the time when she was struggling with the disciples, when she was rebuffed by Jesus, when she encountered one obstacle after another, she could not fully appreciate the deliverance when it occurred. But now that she had a larger, better perspective, she realized that something momentous had occurred for her and her daughter.

Maybe that is the way it is with us, too. We don't always realize the significance of the moment until we reflect on it later. Does the thought sometimes strike you that you are baptized? It happened some time ago, and maybe you remember your feelings then. But now a quiet, deep assurance sinks in when you reflect that you have been identified with Jesus Christ in your baptism.

A worship experience in a church may reap benefits during the week to follow. Perhaps it is only after the saying of prayers that the answers make a home in your spirit. Sometimes you feel nothing, see nothing, experience nothing. But afterward, when sweet reality settles in, you are free to rejoice in what God has given you. When the truth of forgiveness and mercy lights up our previous darkness, we realize that Jesus Christ has actually changed us! And then we know in our hearts that faith is not stupid after all.

The humble will be exalted—nobody else. This will never be our own doing. All is of God. Jesus is the Savior of the world!

"Woman, you have great faith. Your request is granted."

> Leaving that place, Jesus withdrew to the region of Tyre and Sidon. A Canaanite woman from that vicinity came to him, crying out, "Lord, Son of David, have mercy on me! My daughter is suffering terribly from demon-possession."
>
> Jesus did not answer a word. So his disciples came to him and urged him, "Send her away, for she keeps crying after us."
>
> He answered, "I was sent only to the lost sheep of Israel."
>
> The woman came and knelt before him. "Lord, help me!" she said.
>
> He replied, "It is not right to take the children's bread and toss it to their dogs."
>
> "Yes, Lord," she said, "but even the dogs eat the crumbs that fall from their masters' table."
>
> Then Jesus answered, 'Woman, you have great faith! Your request is granted." And her daughter was healed from that very hour.
>
> **Matthew 15:21**

10

Blind Bart

"Move, blind lady," a man hissed at me as he twisted my arm and grabbed my cane. He threw my cane down the escalator, which was taking me to the subway in Washington, D.C. He spat on me and growled, "You people belong in a concentration camp."

I knew that some people dislike those of us with disabilities, but I had no idea that this hostility could take the form of such rabid hatred. . . . I never expected to run up against hate crimes . . . in a respectable, middle-class neighborhood in the United States. But as I wiped the spit from my arm and groped for my cane, I saw what I hadn't seen before: Hatred can break through our fragile bonds of civility.

If my story were unique, I'd shrug it off . . . Disabled people have now become victims of backlash, along with gays, women, minorities, and the elderly. Passage of the Americans with Disabilities Act five years ago created many opportunities for disabled people. This civil rights law, however, has generated resentment. . . . People loved us better when we were pitiable poster children or

167

isolated shut-ins. Now we're a threat, because we can't be turned away from jobs and public accommodations.

Kathi Wolfe, "Opinion Column,"
San Diego Union-Tribune, 2 August 1995.

As Jesus and His disciples, together with a large crowd, were leaving Jericho, a blind man, Bartimaeus (that is, the son of Timaeus), was sitting by the roadside begging. It was a hot day. The wind was blowing softly from the desert. The atmosphere was stifling, and even in the morning hours you could tell it was going to be one of those unbearable days. The sun beat down on you everywhere, especially when you couldn't find a shady spot.

Bart was sitting by the road that started out from Jericho and wound its way to Jerusalem. Yes, he found his usual shady place just outside the city, but that didn't keep him from occasionally having to wipe away the perspiration. This was the only way he could make a living. He was blind and he was unable to work. No one would give him a job. It had been like this for years, and he had learned to accept it. What else could he do but beg?

People were kind. Some dropped in their coins, and some bought the pencils he set in front of him in a wicker basket. And with the little money he received through this small effort, he earned enough to stay alive. It was a meager existence, but he had no complaints, although he never did want to be a liability or a burden to people.

It is really a hardship not being able to see. If you want to know what it feels like, just try walking around with your eyes closed. Without sight, could you hold down your job, shop for groceries, or even make a pot of coffee? When you can't see, your world quickly turns into a dark and dreary place. How much we depend on our eyes every minute of every day; indeed, all of our senses enrich our lives so much!

What if you should lose your sight with no hope of ever regaining it? Can you even bear the thought? You would miss a blessing you now take for granted, and you would realize how precious a gift vision really is. Jesus said, "If your eyes are good, your whole body will be full of light." But what if your eyes are bad? Then your whole existence will be darkness instead of light (Matthew 6:22es, Jesus was talking about spiritual vision, but the illustration is based on physical reality.

Bart couldn't see anything, but he could hear very well; he could tell that people were coming down the road—from the sound of it, a lot of them. Who were all these people? And why were they traveling down this hot road today? What was going on?

Someone had told him that Jesus of Nazareth was in town. Bart had heard stories about Jesus' signs and wonders, about many people whom Jesus had healed.

Some were saying that Jesus was a prophet of God. Some considered Him to be even more than a prophet, possibly a descendent of King David. Was He perhaps the Messiah? Would He reestablish the kingdom to Israel? Had the time come for the Son of David to reign? All sorts of rumors were in the air, and they had reached blind Bart, the beggar by the side of the road from Jericho.

When Bartimaeus heard that it was Jesus of Nazareth, he began to shout, "Jesus, Son of David, have mercy on me!" Many rebuked him and told him to be quiet, but he shouted all the more, "Son of David, have mercy on me!"

But Jesus had not appeared around the bend of the road as yet. That's why those eager people leading the procession insisted that Bart keep quiet. That was a polite way of putting it. Actually, they told him to shut up! "He's not here yet. He's down the road a piece. Don't make such a fuss. Shut your mouth."

"Where is He then?" Bart asked.

"He's on His way. He'll be here, soon."

Son of David—that would mean He is on His way to reign in Jerusalem. So, the Deliverer of Israel, the Son of David is here? Has the time been fulfilled? Will He declare Himself in Jerusalem? Son of David! Son of David, have mercy on me!

Someone had told blind Bart about that day when Jesus entered the synagogue in His home town of Nazareth. The rabbi had asked Him to read from the Prophets, and Jesus had taken the scroll of Isaiah and read, "the Spirit of the Lord is on me, because he has anointed me to preach good news to the poor. He has sent me to proclaim freedom for the prisoners and recovery of sight for the blind" (Luke 4:18). That prophetic Scripture was an announcement of the coming kingdom of God. And blind Bart heard that the Messiah would *open the eyes of the blind*. After rolling up the scroll, Jesus announced to the congregation: "Today this scripture is fulfilled in your hearing" (verse 21).

"Son of David, have mercy on me!" If the Scripture is fulfilled in Jesus of Nazareth, then He can open my eyes too. So Bartimaeus cried out again, only to be met with sounds of "Shhhhh!" But he would not shush, because now Jesus had come around the bend in the road and had reached the place where he was sitting with his pencils.

Jesus stopped and said, "Call him." So they called to the blind man, "Cheer up! On your feet! He's calling you."

Jesus is calling for me? Jesus wants to see me? Is that really possible? Can it be true? The Son of David, the prophet from Nazareth, the healer who has come with power from the Almighty is calling for me? He wants to talk to me? Does that mean I have value? Am I important to him? I thought I had no value. I feel like a reject of society, an outcast, a beggar. I see myself as worthless because I am blind. I'm afflicted and troubled. It's been like that for my whole life. People treat me as if I have the plague. I don't count. And you tell me that Jesus wants to see me? Are you sure?

These were some of the thoughts racing through blind Bart's head when he heard the words, "He's calling you." And these words are for you and me too.

> Jesus calls us from the worship
> Of the vain world's golden store,
> From each idol that would keep us,
> Saying, "Christian, love Me more."
> —*Cecil F. Alexander*

Does Jesus Christ want to see me? Is this really true? Can I believe the good news? Can I overcome my unworthiness? Can I throw out all of my bad thoughts that make me feel unacceptable? It is so hard for me to believe that I am of any value to God. How can I conquer my soul-deep shame, guilt, unworthiness, weaknesses, failures, hurt, and pain? Don't I have to become more worthy before I can feel worthy? Don't I have to make myself acceptable before I can be accepted? Or do you mean to tell me that I can come to Jesus—"just as I am, without one plea," but that His blood was shed for me? I don't have to do anything? Even my unacceptable self has been accepted?

Every one of us is invited to Jesus, for many are called. No one is excluded from His invitation. The light that has come into the world reaches every person. Jesus calls us to enter the kingdom, asks each one of us to believe, to trust, to have hope, and to be saved. Down every road, into every village, into every city, in every country, throughout the whole world Jesus comes calling every one of us. You are invited. You are wanted. If you do not feel worthy, the call of the Lord will make you worthy. If you feel left out, you are assured that you will be included. Ashamed or guilty or whatever your lot, the Lord is calling for the likes of you. No one is left out. No one is to be lost. No one is created for hell. God is not willing that any should perish but that all will come to repentance and faith. The Good Shepherd goes out looking for every lost sheep.

Throwing his cloak aside, Bart jumped to his feet and came to Jesus. Get up! That's all he had to do. Come to Jesus. That's it. Yes, he could do that. That was not a problem for Bart. He was in good physical health. His legs were fine. Everything else about him was OK. It was just that he didn't have his sight. He could even run, if Jesus wanted him to run. Someone offered him an arm and led him to Jesus. He walked along gladly, expectantly, his heart beating wildly in his chest.

"What do you want me to do for you?" Jesus asked him.

What a question! Is Jesus serious? Doesn't He know what I want? Isn't it obvious?

The blind man said, "Rabbi, I want to see."

Bart thought, I don't want to discuss religion with you, sir. I don't have any questions about the existence of God or the creation of the world. I don't even want to discuss the sovereignty of God, the problem of bad things happening to good people, the issue of why I have been afflicted with darkness all my days, nor the reason God allows people like me to suffer so much. Of course I've thought about these things, but that is not why I am here right now. No, sir, I do not want to debate theology. Of course I have questions and concerns, but I've come for another reason.

I believe, Bartimaeus is saying, you are the Master, the Lord, the Son of David. I don't know all that it means, but I believe you have come from God. I can't see you, but I've heard great things about you, *Master*. You have divine power, *Lord*. You can heal people. So I've heard. So I believe. Please, I ask for only one thing. I know I don't have a right to ask for it, but I cannot see now, and I believe you can heal me. I was born with eyes, but I've never been able to use them. If you can touch them, I will be able to see. "Rabbi, I want to see."

Jesus once told His disciples that they were fortunate to be alive. They were more fortunate than the prophets who had predicted the coming of the Messiah. Jesus said, "Blessed are your eyes, because they see, and your ears, because they hear" (Matthew 13:16). Seeing and hearing are often commended in Scripture, especially the seeing and hearing of spiritual truth. Of these two senses, seeing is the more intimate. We greet one another with "Good to see you." Or we say in parting, "I'll be seeing you," or, "See you later." We seldom talk about hearing, because seeing is more personal than hearing. That's why blind Bart wanted to be able to see!

"Go," said Jesus, "your faith has healed you."

Immediately he received his sight. For the first time in his life, his eyes were truly open! What a sensation! What an awakening! He saw the world around him, which he had never seen before. How beautiful it was. How exciting to see earth and sky, mountains and deserts, trees and plants and flowers, a fluttering butterfly—even ants crawling on the ground. And people. So that is what we look like! And Jesus, too, standing there before him. But He was not standing any longer, as if He had to bask in His accomplishments. No, the Son of David was already moving away, moving down the road toward Jerusalem.

Bartimaeus followed Jesus along the road. What was Jesus' purpose for walking to Jerusalem? Why was the Son of David on this journey? Bart decided to follow too. Forget about the pencils. There was nothing to tie him down here. He wanted to see where the road would lead them. Life took on a wonderful new dimension for Bartimaeus. He had been touched and changed, and suddenly he wanted to live this new life to the fullest— wherever that would take him, whatever that would mean—with Jesus.

I draw three conclusions from this simple story.

The first is about faith. "Your faith has healed you." Blind Bart believed, and that faith brought about his healing—not much faith, possibly, but enough. It did not take much faith to be made whole. Only a grain of mustard seed is enough to begin new growth in a life. And now Bart was able to see after all those years—his sight confirmed his faith. Because of his new vision he realized that he had faith before he was given the gift of sight. Faith made him call out to Jesus, and the healing verified blind Bart's faith. He had been touched and changed.

Faith brought him to sight. Now that sight confirmed his faith.

It was faith not in faith nor in the gift of sight nor in the pursuit of his goals. It was purely and simply faith in God. That is what faith is about. Faith is always in God. When we put our faith in someone, it is usually for two reasons: 1) We believe that this person is trustworthy, someone of integrity; we expect the person to be there for us. 2) We expect this person to do what we have asked. We believe that this person is able to do what we ask. So our faith is twofold, we believe in the integrity and in the competence of that person. Faith in God is a trust in our Creator-Redeemer, in the nature of the living, holy, merciful, righteous God, and in God's ability and competence to keep His promises.

That is why blind Bart's faith is in Jesus, the Son of David, the Son of God, the Messiah, the Lord of life, not in some sort of magic. This man from Nazareth has divine power over sickness and disease. His power is from God. The Son of David has come from God to heal and to save His people.

For all of us who sit by life's road defeated by our trials, burdened by our cares, and overwhelmed by our suffering, Jesus comes with healing power. When we call out for Him, we are not ignored. He takes notice of us. He even calls us to come to Him, invites us to pray and approach Him with all our pain. Jesus is here to bless and receive us. And faith responds to that call. "Your faith has healed you." That's the first observation.

The second is that blind Bart did not give up. They told him to shush, but he would not be quiet. He was persistent. He would not take no for an answer. If Jesus, the Son of David was indeed here in Jericho this one and only time, then there was no stopping Bartimaeus.

When you have a physical affliction, that need not be the end of your life. You do not need to give up. Whatever the problem—physical, mental, or spiritual—there is never a good reason for you to abandon your pursuit of God. It is so easy to throw in the towel, but why do that?

"Well, I have never really had an experience of God, why should I keep hoping? It's no use. I believe in Jesus, that He died for me on the cross and rose from the dead. But I have never had a revelation like other people have. How can I be sure God is there at all? How can I be convinced that God is interested in me? My life has been nothing but drudgery and duty. I've never had a vision. I've never seen an angel. I've never had an experience of God or felt Him in the way other people say they have."

It is easy to throw up your hands and quit. Like Bartimaeus, you are blind and you have never seen God. And you don't expect to. The doors have been shut, and you are locked out. But, like Bartimaeus, don't quit now. Keep on calling to Jesus. Don't stop. There is hope for you.

Perhaps you feel defeated. You have failed, and your failure has left a residue of misery. You feel let down. Perhaps you have been through a divorce, and you consider that a monumental failure. You have lost a job not for the reasons you have given people but because of your own negligence. And you know it. If the truth were known, it was your fault that you were let go. Or you have blown a great opportunity in life because of your weakness. You were tempted and did not resist temptation. Now you might as well give up. Redemption? There is no redemption for you because you've blown it. It's no use. It's too late.

It is not too late. No matter how badly you have messed up your life, Jesus Christ offers pardon and renewal. There is no sin that Jesus will not forgive if you ask Him in sincerity and truth, if you come with all your heart. No matter what roadblocks have been put in your way, do not quit, keep calling out to Jesus.

Now the third conclusion is this: After you have demonstrated faith and refused to give up, you still can do one more thing. You can cry out for help. You can call out to the Son of David, the Lord of life. You can ask Him to have mercy on you. You can pray. You may have lost your sight, but you haven't lost your voice or any other faculties. You can ask in Jesus' name, and when you ask, Jesus promises that you will be heard. You can believe the promise, that "Everyone who calls on the name of the Lord will be saved" (Romans 10:13). That invitation is broad enough to include you.

You may not be able to see your way ahead, but you can accept the truth, you can believe in the Lord, you can commit your life to Him. All your senses are still intact. You can reason and you can feel. The problem is that when we lose something we see only our losses. We cannot concentrate on anything else. We focus on the loss of our vision, whether it's physical or spiritual. Instead of concentrating so much on the loss, can we select what we have left?—which is more than enough to call on the name of the Lord, as blind Bart did, and so be saved.

Seize the moment. This is the day the Lord has made. This very day. The time is now. "Today if you hear his voice, do not harden your hearts" (Hebrews 4:7). This day can be a day of new beginnings. This day need not be a clone of yesterday. It is a new creation of God, and therefore today lies before you as a newborn child—something wonderful, something good. It is not a repeat of the past. You can expect God to be in today with you and for you and in you. Seize the moment!

All Jesus asks of us is to believe, like blind Bart. Again and again Jesus has demonstrated His ability to save and to heal. Isn't that enough for us? Isn't that enough to trust Him with our woeful blindness and our wayward ways? to confess our sins, our failures and our weaknesses? to ask for healing and to believe in the healing that comes from our Savior?

This simple story of blind Bart is here for my encouragement. It builds my faith. It helps me to discover and act on my need for God. It lifts me above my pain and suffering and gives me hope in the salvation Jesus brings. And it assures me that when I call out to Him, Jesus has already come calling for me! "Jesus stopped and said, 'Call him.' So they called to the blind man, 'Cheer up! On your feet! He's calling you!'"

I could never find Him if He had not already searched me out. Jesus is sent from the Father into the world to find the lost sheep. He comes calling for you and for me. And when I come, believing, I will be received with all my sins, all my failures, all my weaknesses, all my losses. And not only received, but welcomed, saved, touched, healed, and transformed!

> Just as I am, without one plea
> But that Thy blood was shed for me,
> . . . .
> O Lamb of God, I come! I come!
> —*Charlotte Elliott*

They came to Jericho. As Jesus and his disciples, together with a large crowd, were leaving the city, a blind man, Bartimaeus (that is, the Son of Timaeus), was sitting by the roadside begging. When he heard that it was Jesus of Nazareth, he began to shout, "Jesus, Son of David, have mercy on me!"

Many rebuked him and told him to be quiet, but he shouted all the more, "Son of David, have mercy on me!"

"Jesus stopped and said, "Call him."

So they called to the blind man, "Cheer up! On your feet! He's calling you." Throwing his cloak aside, he jumped to his feet and came to Jesus.

"What do you want me to do for you?" Jesus asked him.

The blind man said, "Rabbi, I want to see."

"Go," said Jesus, "your faith has healed you."

Immediately he received his sight and followed Jesus along the road.

Mark 10:46

The Donkey Man

I had heard about this Nazarene, but not very much. The news from Galilee filtered down to our little village, but it was sparse. Stories have a way of making the rounds, but you never know how much they've changed by the time you hear them. You don't always know what to believe, so you pick and choose, I suppose. And so I picked and chose what to believe about Jesus. For example, can I believe that Jesus is able to walk on water? I know from experience that the human body sinks into water. How then can the body of Jesus keep from being submerged? I'd like to see that for myself! I ask you, can you believe someone is able to walk on water? Have you ever seen anyone do that?

Someone told me about a man who wanted to experiment, after he had heard about this miracle of Jesus. This man gathered up some flat rocks and positioned them just below the surface of a shallow pond. He thought he had arranged them so that only he could tell where the stones were. They were not visible from shore. Then he invited some people to watch him as he announced he would walk on the water. So he stepped out on the rocks he had laid in the pond, but his deception was obvious. They laughed at him as he made his way across. Their laughter so flustered him that he lost his balance and fell in! Served him right.

So, did Jesus actually walk on water? The reporters swear to it. They are convinced because they have talked with the disciples who witnessed the happening on the lake. Though they insist the story is true, who is to know? I've also heard many stories about Jesus' healing touch. I cannot reject them since they have been verified. You would have to be an ostrich with its head in the sand to deny the evidence. Jesus is a gifted and amazing prophet of God. But I'm getting ahead of my story.

I live in Bethany, a small and quiet town just outside of Jerusalem. Picture a simple, pleasant, newer housing development. The homes on our street are all pretty much the same size, nothing fancy. I have a white picket fence around the property, a little backyard, and a small animal shelter. You see, we travel by donkey or oxcart, and we keep our animals in shelters. Some of the more affluent among us have camels or three or four donkeys for transportation. I had only one donkey, a very old one. His days of usefulness were over. So I bought myself a young colt. This colt had recently been taken from the mare and had never been ridden. I was waiting for the day, probably in a week or less, when I would break him in. He seemed to be a fine animal. I was looking forward to that day.

Well, let me tell you what happened. One morning as I was picking up the paper, two men came walking down our street eyeing our homes and properties. I didn't know whether they were spying out our neighborhood with the intention of robbing us when we were gone or what they had in mind. They were strangers to me, and I know practically everybody in Bethany. It's a small town.

I was watching as they walked straight up to my house—yes, my house. My new colt was tied to the fence just inside the gate. He was grazing, and they started to untie the rope. They were going to take my donkey as I watched. Just like that!

"Hey, what do you think you're doing?" I asked.

"We're untying this colt."

"Well, you can just stop that. That's my animal."

"Yes, we suppose that is true," they said, and they sounded very polite, "but we are about to take it. We need it."

"Well, you can't just take it. It's my animal. My transportation. My property. It doesn't belong to you!"

"We know that, but we want this animal," they insisted.

I raised my voice. "But you can't just take it from me, now can you? You can't have it. That's stealing, and the law says, 'You shall not steal.'"

They didn't budge. "We are not stealing this colt, we are only going to borrow him for a little while," they said firmly.

"What's the difference? If you take him you are stealing, even if you call it borrowing."

In the meantime some neighbors had gathered, hearing all this commotion. They formed a circle around us. Soon, the strangers were outnumbered.

"Let us tell you the reason why we are doing this."

"You have a reason?"

"Yes. The Lord has need of this colt."

"What do you mean, the Lord?"

"There is only one Lord."

"Yes, we agree on that. But what are you talking about?"

"Jesus."

"Jesus who?"

"Jesus of Nazareth!"

"You mean *the* Jesus of Nazareth?"

"Exactly."

"I've heard stories about His miracles," I said.

"Good," they replied. "Because then

you'll understand that Jesus wants this animal for a good cause."

"What good cause?" I asked.

"We really don't know the answer to that. He didn't tell us. All Jesus told us to do is to find a colt and bring it to Him."

"Well, now, who is this Jesus of Nazareth?"

"Jesus is the Lord."

"What does that mean?"

"It means that He is the Promised One, the Messiah. He comes in the name of the Lord. He has come from God."

"Hmmm," I said. "And you say that Jesus wants *my* donkey?"

"That's right."

"How do you know He wants *this* donkey?"

"We don't know that. We don't know why."

"So why mine? Can't you take somebody else's? This is a very young colt."

"Has anyone ever ridden this colt before?"

"No. Not yet. I am going to break him in tomorrow as a matter of fact."

"Well then, this is the one He wants."

"Why?"

"Because no one has ridden this donkey."

"That doesn't make sense," I replied. "I don't understand."

"You're not supposed to understand," they said. "We don't always understand what the Lord has in mind either. He told us to find a young colt that had never been ridden, and He didn't say why. But He assured us that we will be returning this donkey to you on the same day."

"You mean He only wants it for one day?"

"That's right."

"You will have it back here before nightfall?"

"We promise that."

I shook my head. I didn't know what to think. "All right then," I said flatly.

I didn't have them sign papers. It didn't seem necessary somehow. I mean, this is not a rental. All I can do is to take their word for it.

My wife missed most of this conversation. She didn't hear what was happening out front. She was busy somewhere in the back of the house. But now she was standing out by the fence and I quickly filled her in with some of the details.

"Well, let's go and see where they're leading our colt," she said. "Come on, let's follow them right now, before they get out of sight."

That's when we hurried after them out of Bethany. We soon came to the main road that takes you straight into Jerusalem.

Jesus was there, waiting for us. He mounted the colt and gently prodded the animal to move. We watched as He prepared to enter the city. He sat astride the donkey—my new young donkey—and led the parade.

The disciples were exultant. They walked with Him excitedly and energized, feeling very important, smiling at the gathering crowd along the way. Children entered the parade with wild shouts and innocent delight. People joined in from everywhere, tearing palm branches from trees, laying them down on that last stretch of road that takes you right up to the city gate.

"Blessed is he who comes in the name of the Lord!" "Hosanna in the highest!" People were shouting and singing, and all the while Jesus rode calmly but majestically on my donkey to Jerusalem. On my donkey! I couldn't take my eyes off him.

He did not ride into the city on a horse or a camel as a ruler or potentate might do. A proud animal usually brings a person of importance and is certainly more fit for a king. But Jesus did not act like an important person might act. He had chosen a young colt, a symbol of humility, to present Himself to the city. He did not wave at the people like a politician will do. He did not nod or smile condescendingly. He did not seem to be swayed by the shouting of the enthusiasts. He was not mesmerized by the

crowd. It seemed as if His focus was else-
where, on something that lay before Him.
His destiny was there in Jerusalem not only
on this very day, but in the days to come.

It was as if He realized He would be
rejected by the authorities and would suffer terrible pain in body, mind, and spirit.
His eyes seemed focused on the outcome of
this visit to Jerusalem, and a kind of
peaceful acceptance—no anxiety or fear—
shone from His face. His compassion and
mercy seemed to encompass people. I must
tell you that I didn't really understand all
this while we were entering the city, even
though I am describing it to you now. Only
later as I reflected on the triumphal journey did I realize what I had been seeing. I
was so glad we joined in the procession.

Entering by the city gate, we headed
straight for the temple grounds. Jesus
knew He was going there, but not many
people followed the parade to its conclusion. A few were still with us when we
reached the temple. As far as my donkey
was concerned, I saw the disciples tie the
animal up somewhere nearby, but I followed Jesus because I wanted to listen to
His teaching in the temple. Momentarily,
my wife and I forgot about the animal. He
was safe.

I saw Jesus tie some ropes together,
and then He lashed out at the money
changers. He forcibly upended their tables

with all their papers and money, drove out the animals, and cleared the temple grounds. "This is a house of prayer," I heard Him shout. "You have made it a den for robbers." There was general confusion—people sprinting here and there, the priests scurrying for cover, the animals bleating and screeching, running wild and frightened. My wife and I just watched the spectacle from a distance, wondering what to make of the hectic display in that holy place!

When things quieted down a little, we returned home—but without the donkey. Someone must have taken the animal somewhere, but that didn't matter. We had been assured that they would return it later.

They brought back my colt before nightfall just as they promised. The animal seemed perfectly all right, none the worse for wear. I examined it carefully while the disciples watched. They thanked me again for allowing the Lord to ride it.

"By the way, I don't even know your names," I said.

"Oh, yes," one answered, "but that's not important. Anyway, I'm Philip and this is my friend Nathanael."

What an honor it is to ride my donkey now! Wherever I travel on my colt, I think, *The Lord rode my colt into Jerusalem!* I cannot explain the spiritual sensation when I comprehend this truth. "Hosanna to the Son of David!" "Blessed is he who comes in the name of the Lord!" "Hosanna in the highest!" I ride on the very same animal that transported our King into the Holy City!

Sometimes I reflect on an old Bible story, the one about the prophet Balaam and his donkey. Balaam was asked by the king of Moab to curse the Israelites. When Balaam refused, the king sent a larger entourage and offered more gifts—bribes— so Balaam reluctantly relented. The prophet was traveling down a certain road but didn't recognize the angel of the Lord who stood, sword in hand, blocking the way. Balaam's donkey saw the angel and veered into the field. Balaam struck the donkey and prodded it back to the road. Once again the donkey stopped and was beaten. The beast even dropped to the ground and when the angry prophet struck him again, the Lord miraculously gave the donkey speech, and the donkey asked why he was being treated this way when he had served the prophet faithfully for years! Then Balaam saw the angel standing in the way with his sword drawn.

I don't have any idea how that animal was able to talk, but I wish the Lord would make my donkey speak too. I'd like to know what it was like for him to carry the Son of David into the holy city, to transport the Savior of Israel. Oh, well. . . . Oh, and by the way, Balaam did not curse the Israelites.

All of this has made me a better person. I have learned that something I valued, my new colt, could become a very serious test for me when I am asked to offer it to Jesus. This is not an easy thing to do. We do not relinquish possessions readily, especially when it's something dear to us. I was very reluctant to offer that sacrifice for God. But the truth is that Jesus returns our gifts after we have released them. What I found troublesome to dedicate to Him, He has given back with His blessing. And suddenly my ordinary colt seems different, yes, more exciting to ride.

I realize that this is also true of other things. Some religious people speak of making commitments to the Lord. They encourage the making of vows to God. Some offer special gifts on the altar. Some dedicate their lives to the Lord. Some even take vows of celibacy or, if not that, promises of fidelity. They promise to remain pure before marriage and faithful in marriage. Others take vows of poverty. They will not surround themselves with things and set their hearts on earthly possessions. The vow of obedience is a promise to follow the Lord.

God accepts our gifts and sees our commitment. Then He renews our souls.

He gives us freely of His Spirit and thereby provides the power that can turn us into better persons. I certainly feel that my life has taken a turn for the better because I offered my colt to the disciples on that day. Well, there was a little pressure, you understand, or probably I wouldn't have donated the animal. But having presented my donkey, I received back more than my donkey! I received a new life, a deepening of spiritual experience. This would not have happened if I had kept the animal tied up in my yard.

As you can probably tell, that was not the end of my involvement with Jesus. My wife and I returned to Jerusalem every day during that week. We listened to His teaching. We wanted to know more about the kingdom of God. We were caught up by His stories, the parables, as He called them. We heard Him debate theology with some of our religious leaders. They asked Him impossible questions, and He responded with the most profound answers.

We were in the city on Friday morning after His arrest. We arrived a little late for the entire trial, because there had been no advance publicity. It all happened so fast. We joined the crowd as Jesus was already standing before Pilate. We heard the shouting and screaming and the demand for the release of Barabbas. Barabbas was a popular freedom fighter. He was a Zealot who hoped to overthrow the Romans and establish the kingdom rule of Israel. He had been arrested by the Romans because he killed some of their soldiers. Pilate presented both Jesus and Barabbas to the crowd, one on either side of him. We couldn't do anything to change the mood of the people once they shouted for Barabbas's freedom; we couldn't stop the destruction of Jesus. Barabbas was released, and Jesus was sent to His death.

We followed silently to the place where they hanged Him, on a cross between two thieves. We stood and watched the terrible proceedings. I wish I could forget that day, but I cannot. While others mocked, we prayed. While others laughed, we cried. The horrendous scene lives on in my memory. It was only later that I understood the significance of His death.

But one week after Jesus had entered Jerusalem on my colt, in the afternoon of that day, my wife and I heard rumors of a resurrection! What incredible news! What an unbelievable story—the tomb where they laid Him is empty, and Jesus is supposed to have reappeared from the dead? We had never heard anything like that before—not in the history of our nation, not about anyone else. Not any of the fathers of Israel, not any of our prophets reappeared from the grave. No one. And Jesus is suddenly alive? He is not dead?

We returned to Jerusalem to verify the story. Many of the earlier miracles I had heard about were accomplished in Galilee, but the resurrection took place right under our noses here in Judea! The report said that Jesus actually walked away from the tomb in which He had been placed. He had been lifeless, but He came back to life. We heard that on this very day Jesus disclosed Himself to some of His disciples— first to some women, then to the men—revealed Himself as the living Savior!

We went to see Philip and Nathanael, who had taken our colt a week earlier. They were hiding out somewhere in the city, but we located them and asked them about these reports. Was the story true? Was it possible? Had Jesus actually revealed Himself to them? Had they seen Him too? Could they confirm this? When they recognized us from the week before, they assured us that it was all gloriously true.

The resurrection verified the disciples' faith, sealed it for them. They related much more. There were stories circulating around Jerusalem that the authorities had bribed the soldiers to falsify their reports. The Jewish leaders were blaming the empty tomb on Jesus' followers and let it be known that His disciples had robbed the tomb and stolen the body, and many such wild and fanciful tales.

Then, I asked why Jesus had to suffer so on the cross? What was the purpose of that shameful death? Why did the promised Messiah, the Son of David, endure such misery? Isn't the Messiah supposed to reign on the throne of David as our king? Why are all those prophetic promises not now fulfilled?

They informed us that Jesus had often predicted His crucifixion as well as His resurrection. They could not understand Him at first either. Now, looking back, they began to put the pieces together. They now realize why Jesus had predicted these events.

We Jews believe in the necessity of sacrifice for our redemption. We understand about sacrifice and atonement, about sheep and goats slain for our sins. Atonement is achieved only through the shedding of blood. Jesus, like a sacrificial lamb, would have to give His life to make atonement for our sins. To redeem us once and for all, Jesus had to suffer such an excruciating death. By His substitutionary death He would save us. By taking our sin upon Him, He would set us free. As John the Baptist had announced when Jesus offered Himself to be baptized: "Look, the Lamb of God who takes away the sin of the world" (John 1:29).

Jesus paid the ransom. The Lamb of God took our sin that we might be set free.

He accepted the judgment that we might not be condemned. He paid the price for our redemption.

We had witnessed the death of the Son of God on the cross—nothing less than that! He is not only a good man and beloved teacher, He is the Holy One of God. And that is what takes our breath away, when we behold the one who died for us. As one of the apostles, our friend Paul, told us later: "God made him who had no sin to be sin for us, so that in him we might become the righteousness of God" (2 Corinthians 5:21).

The resurrection confirms our faith. The glorious triumph of the Son of David assures us of the victory of God over Satan, of life over death. We went home with joyful hearts. Our time of sorrow had turned into deep, inner joy.

Yes. Every time I ride my donkey I think of Jesus not only as triumphant King, but also as suffering Savior. And risen Lord. And I feel peaceful.

All of that happened long ago. I'm older now, and so is my donkey. We don't ride him anymore. He just grazes in the backyard. Every time I look at him, I remember the day of the royal procession when the Lord had need of him.

As for me, Jesus has touched and changed my life too. I can't begin to tell you. My words are poor, but I assure you that my heart is warm, my faith is firm, and my life is changed. The Spirit is making a difference in the way I think. I have a tendency to be anxious and worried about things. I still battle anxiety, but I am more at ease. I even feel calm. When things go wrong I can quite naturally fall into discouragement, even become a little depressed. That doesn't happen to me like it used to. Because of my faith I experience hope—hope in God. And I don't mean only a hope in life eternal but also for right now.

Yes, I'm happy the Lord chose my donkey on that fateful day. And I'm happy that the Lord chose me, too, for His kingdom.

As [Jesus] approached Bethphage and Bethany at the hill called the Mount of Olives, he sent two of his disciples, saying to them, "Go to the village ahead of you, and as you enter it, you will find a colt tied there, which no one has ever ridden. Untie it and bring it here. If anyone asks you, 'Why are you untying it?' tell him, 'The Lord needs it.'"

Those who were sent ahead went and found it just as he had told them. As they were untying the colt, its owners asked them, "Why are you untying the colt?"

They replied, "The Lord needs it."

They brought it to Jesus, threw their cloaks on the colt and put Jesus on it. As he went along, people spread their cloaks on the road.

When he came near the place where the road goes down the Mount of Olives, the whole crowd of disciples began joyfully to praise God in loud voices for all the miracles they had seen:

"Blessed is the king who comes in the name of the Lord!"

"Peace in heaven and glory in the highest!" . . .

As he approached Jerusalem and saw the city he wept over it. . . . Then he entered the temple area and began driving out those who were selling. "It is written," he said to them, "'My house will be a house of prayer'; but you have made it 'a den of robbers.'"

Luke 19:29

A Final Word

If you have shared in this journey of faith with these people whom Jesus touched and changed, where does that leave you? Have you felt the need for Jesus to affect your life? to bring you healing, wholeness, peace, forgiveness, joy, hope, love—whatever you need?

You see, it really doesn't matter where you've been or what you've done, nor does it matter how you may be feeling at this moment. You may be as righteous and law-abiding as Nicodemus or as sinful as the woman who came to Jacob's well. You may be troubled by a situation that has you baffled like the blue lady, or you may even be possessed like the man among the tombs. You may be unaware of your spiritual condition, like the disabled man brought by four friends. You may be as helpless as the lost soul waiting by the pool in Jerusalem or as powerful as the synagogue leader whose daughter was dying.

No matter who you are or where you are at this moment, you can come to Jesus. Or better yet, you can believe that Jesus comes to you! That is why Jesus entered the world in the first place—to seek and to save the lost. That is why He is here with us to the end of the age. He sees you, knows you, cares about you and wants to heal you. The gospel stories focus on a single truth. They are faith stories of salvation that profoundly changes lives—a wonderful salvation that is available to you!

But what if you have already accepted Jesus as your Savior? What if you are a believer? That must not keep you from being touched again! Yes, you may be assured of your salvation. You may know you are going to heaven, but does that mean that you no longer need anything else? Have you received every blessing of God? Surely you do not think you have already arrived at the pearly gates.

No matter how long or how short a time you have been a Christian, Jesus magnetizes us all: "I, when I am lifted up from the earth, will draw all men to myself" (John 12:32). This very moment you can experience His touch. We all need to be "conformed to the likeness of God's Son" (Romans 8:29).

I myself entered the narrow way forty-nine years ago. I have traveled the road, but sometimes poorly, sometimes going astray in the fields only to return with confession and repentance. I made my initial commitment years ago, but I have needed to renew my devotion many times since. I will need to be touched and changed anew until I reach the end of the way.

What, then, do we have to do? What can we do?

• Come to Jesus, as did old Nick, even if you have to approach Him under the cover of darkness.

• If you can't make it on your own, allow your friends to bring you, just as the friends of Joe brought him on a pallet to Jesus.

• Call out to Jesus, no matter how many people block your way; blind Bart did that.

• Persist no matter how often you may be rebuffed or rejected, like the alien who was determined to pursue her quest.

• Have faith like the centurion.

• Reach out and touch Jesus, believing, as the blue lady who touched His clothing.

• Let Him reveal your secrets, in the assurance that He will fully accept you! That is how Jesus accepted the Samaritan woman at the well!

• Let Jesus forgive your sins as He forgave the disabled man who thought he was there only for his disability.

• When Jesus touches something deep within you, tell Him you want to be made whole, just like the lost soul by the pool in Jerusalem who walked away after thirty-eight years of misery.

• Let Jesus cast out the demons that have controlled you.

• Give Jesus whatever He may ask, as did the donkey man.

Jesus touched and changed others. He wants to do the same for you! And He can!

Note to the Reader

The publisher invites you to share your response to the message of this book by writing Discovery House Publishers, Box 3566, Grand Rapids, MI 49501, USA. For information about other Discovery House books, music, or videos, contact us at the same address or call 1-800-653-8333. Find us on the Internet at http://www.dhp.org/ or send e-mail to books@dhp.org.